The Lamb

The Lamb

Sermons for the Easter Cycle
from Pentecost to Ash Wednesday

Frederick W. Kemper

Publishing House
St. Louis

Concordia Publishing House, St. Louis, Missouri
Copyright © 1983 Concordia Publishing House

Manufactured in the United States of America

Library of Congress Cataloging in Publication Data

Kemper, Frederick W.
    The lamb.

    Includes index.
      1. Lutheran Church—Sermons.   2. Church year sermons.
3. Sermons, American.   I. Title.
BX8066.K38L35 1983   252'.62   82-25237
ISBN 0-570-03901-0 (pbk.)

---

1 2 3 4 5 6 7 8 9 10 WP 92 91 90 89 88 87 86 85 84 83

**To Ruth and Anna,
both saints in time**

Contents

Foreword

Scripture is its own star witness to the inspiration of the Holy Spirit, who moved holy men to write it. It is amazing enough to be classed with the miraculous that about thirty-six men should have written its sixty-six books over a period of about sixteen centuries in three different languages and about six different countries—and have them come out as a cohesive whole. There is no question about the Spirit's guiding hand.

The Bible is like an artesian well drawing water from deep in the heart of God. It is a veritable Solomon's mine, deep in the mind of God, filled with buried treasures free to all who will dig deep to search them out. People spend lifetimes being students of the Scripture, studying the sacred Word, only to discover there was not enough time to gather the gems or exhaust the precious veins.

Take, for instance, the motifs that run through the holy writings. Prophecy and fulfillment is one such motif, as the Old Testament gives up its mysteries in the New. Notice the recurring sin, judgment, grace rhythm that begins in Genesis and is still strong in Revelation. Study the covenant motif, starting with Adamitic through the Sinaitic, into the New Covenant "in My blood" of the upper room. There are many more, some coursing through the whole of Scripture, some limited to "areas"; and each has its own fascination.

I was put onto and enamored of the Lamb motif by J. Sidlow Baxter, who developed the theme in a volume entitled *The Master Theme of the Bible*. Some of his discovery and thinking may inadvertently be reflected in these sermons. However, once having found the theme in his work, I elected to embellish it in my own way. Needless to say, I am grateful to him for his leading me into the "mine" and showing me where to look for the treasure.

The theme is not exhausted in these sermons, first preached at Galilee Lutheran Church on the eastern shore of Maryland. Nor is the treatment as profound as it might be in a different kind of work. Sermons are for the lay people and are written and preached for convicting and convincing. They therefore have to have a certain simplicity while they hint at the deeper things available for the mining.

The series extends to and includes Pentecost, for Easter is not a one-day celebration but a state of mind, a condition of the Spirit. The story of the Lamb is not finished with these excursions into the motif. There is still room for the adventurous preacher. The isolation of these texts seemed enough for this series.

The Scriptures come to our generation from another kind of culture. It is quite remarkable that concepts like king and vine, miracle and sacrifice, sheep and shepherd should still be vivid to us. Yet such concepts live, and in them Jesus is revealed to us in His majesty, His power, His tenderness. The Holy Spirit, Mover of holy men, truly had us and our salvation in mind, when He honed His tools for gathering together a church for the glory and praise of God.

Lent

1. In the Beginning, the Lamb (Ash Wednesday)

Suggested Hymns
    A Lamb goes uncomplaining forth
    Lamb of God, pure and holy
    Come to Calvary's holy mountain
    Round me falls the night

Suggested Scripture
    Matthew 26:14-35
    Genesis 4:1-16
    The interwoven Passion story

Suggested Psalm
    Psalm 130

A Litany for Ash Wednesday

(Litany: A resonant or repetitive recital or chant)

Pastor: All we like sheep have gone astray: We have turned every one to
    his own way;
People: And the Lord has laid on Him the iniquity of us all.
Pastor: When Eve saw the tree was good for food, she took of its fruit and
    ate. And she also gave some to Adam, and he ate.
People: All we like sheep have gone astray;
Pastor: Noah planted a vineyard; and he drank of the wine, and became
    drunk and lay uncovered in his tent.
People: We have turned every one to his own way;
Pastor: Abraham said to Sarah, Say you are my sister, that it may go well
    with me because of you, and that my life may be spared on your
    account.
People: And the Lord has laid on Him the iniquity of us all.
Pastor: Moses went out to his people and looked on their burdens; and he
    saw an Egyptian beating a Hebrew. He looked this way and that, and
    seeing no one, he killed the Egyptian and hid him in the sand.

People: All we like sheep have gone astray;

Pastor: King David arose from his couch and was walking upon the roof of the king's house. He saw from the roof a woman bathing, and the woman was very beautiful. David sent messengers and took her.

People: We have turned every one to his own way;

Pastor: Zachariah said to the angel, "How shall I know this? for I am an old man, and my wife is advanced in years." And the angel answered him, "You will be silent and unable to speak until the day that these things come to pass, because you did not believe my words."

People: And the Lord has laid on Him the iniquity of us all.

Pastor: Jesus arose from prayer and found them sleeping for sorrow. "Could you not watch with Me one hour? . . . Judas, would you betray the Son of Man with a kiss?" . . . And Peter denied it, saying, "Woman, I do not know Him."

People: All we like sheep have gone astray;

Pastor: Out of the heart proceed evil thought, murders, adulteries, fornications, thefts, false witness, blasphemies.

People: We have gone every one to his own way;

Pastor: Jesus said, "Father forgive them, for they know not what they do."

People: And the Lord has laid on Him the iniquity of us all.

Pastor: What then shall we say to this? If God is for us, who is against us?

People: And the Lord has laid on Him the iniquity of us all.

Pastor: Who shall bring any charge against God's elect?

People: And the Lord has laid on Him the iniquity of us all.

Pastor: Who shall separate us from the love of God?

People: And the Lord has laid on Him the iniquity of us all.

Pastor: I am sure that neither death, nor life, nor angels, nor principalities, nor things present, nor things to come, nor powers, nor height, nor depth, nor anything else in all creation, will be able to separate us from the love of God in Christ Jesus our Lord.

People: For the Lord has laid on Him the iniquity of us all, and with His stripes we are healed.

In the Beginning, the Lamb

Text: Genesis 4:4-16 (Genesis 4:4)

Dear Friends of Christ,

All things, save God, have a genesis, a beginning. God alone is eternal, without beginning, without end. In Him, under Him, through Him, all things have *their* beginning.

In sheer inspiration, the holy writer began the Scriptures with measured, mighty, majestic words.

"In the beginning God created the heavens and the earth."

Out of the darkness, in the darkness, with a powerful word, the world was called into being.

"Let there be light," He said, and there was light.

"Let there be grasses, and birds, and fishes and animals," and the barren earth, at His command, was foliated and graced with life in the sea and air and upon the earth.

And God saw that it was good.

Genesis: In the beginning, the creating God formed man of the dust of the ground. He blew the breath of life from deep within Himself into man. And man became a living soul.

Genesis: In the beginning, God formed the woman from a part of Adam. He set the man and the woman into the lush garden of Eden. He led them to a certain tree, known as the tree of the knowledge of good and evil. He forbade them to eat of that one tree alone, of all the trees in the garden. Adam and Eve luxuriated in their Paradise. Every turn on every walk brought new discovery and new excitement. They reveled in the sunshine; they danced in the rain; they slept without fear in the night.

Genesis: In the beginning, Satan, a fallen angel of light, came tempting the primal pair. He chose the form of the serpent for his seduction. As a serpent he hung in graceful loops from the forbidden tree. With cunning words he created doubts about the authority of the Creator and the limitations placed on the creature. Adam and Eve reached for the fruit of the forbidden tree and "did eat of it."

Genesis. The beginning of sin.

The beginning of the rupture in the relation, in the fellowship of the creature with his Creator, of man with God.

Genesis. The discovery of God in His justice and judgment.

God cursed the serpent, "Upon your belly you shall crawl, and dust you shall eat."

Genesis. The promise of the Savior, who would right the wrong of Adam, who would crush the power of Satan. "You, Satan, and the Son of the woman will be enemies. You will strike at His heel, but He will crush your head!"

Genesis. God speaks the Good News . . . in the hearing of Adam and Eve.

Eve will bear children, and of these children One will conquer Satan and all his power, all he stands for.

Hope is born into the world.

Faith is born into the world.

God has spoken, and the word is grace, and forgiveness, and reconciliation.

Whatever God would say now to Adam and to Eve, the Good News was there to temper it.

17

Let God speak in judgment to Eve. The promise came first!

Let God speak in judgment to Adam. The Good News preceded it!

At every birth for thousands of years, women would wonder . . . is this the Promised Seed?

At every human birth Satan would tremble: Is this He who is to crush My head?

Out of the garden into the world, God sent his creatures. They looked back at the gates and saw an angel with a flaming sword.

They could not return. All mankind could not return. Paradise was forfeited . . . but hope had been born in the promises of God.

Genesis. A child is born, Cain, the firstborn.

His birth brought excitement and hope.

Eve thought surely the promise was fulfilled, that the little infant boy was the Child of the promise.

Satan trembled as he wondered if this was the Enemy of the curse.

In due course the second son was born. They named him Abel.

Cain was proud of his place and position as firstborn.

He enjoyed the privileges of the firstborn given him by his parents.

He was given the more important task of tilling the soil.

He had a tendency to dominate his brother.

When the family gathered of an evening, the day's chores finished, Adam told and retold the story of the beginnings.

Cain listened, enthralled with how it all came about . . . seed bearing fruit and fruit bearing seed after its own kind . . . the birds, the animals, the fish reproducing themselves.

He had turned off the stories of how they had been expelled from the garden. The story degraded his parents. He determined not to think about it.

It was enough that there was an explanation for the beginning of all budding fruit trees, the fascinating animals, the garden of vegetables he cultivated. As long as God maintained the sunshine and the rain, he was quite content.

Abel grew up in his older brother's shadow.

As Cain assumed his prerogatives as firstborn, Abel accepted his lesser role as second son.

He heard the same stories Cain heard.

He found fascination in the story of the serpent, and Adam's sin, and above all in the promise and the assurance that the power of the evil one would be destroyed one day.

To him was assigned the shepherd's task.

He appreciated the opportunity the long hours, alone with his grazing flock, gave him for meditation.

The promise surged into his thinking again and again.

And as often as he meditated on it, he wondered about the time of its fulfillment.

Genesis. The beginning of worship, the response of man to his God.

Cain gathered a basket of luscious fruits from his trees, and grain heavy with seed from his fields.

He set them before the altar, full of gratitude for the generosity of God.

It was his way of thanking the Creator and Preserver for His blessings of the farmed land.

His thankoffering was indeed laudable; his motive of gratitude was indeed high.

But he did not have the faith God wanted; his faith was supplanted by his self-importance as firstborn.

God did not look with favor on Cain and his offering.

For his offering on that fatal day, Abel chose a lamb.

He picked with great care.

If he was to bring an acceptable offering to the Giver of the promise, only the best of his flocks would do.

Abel knew he was a child of Adam. He knew and understood that, far more than the flesh-ties, the sin of his parents were his as well.

He offered his lamb with the prayer that the promise might soon be fulfilled, that he would be faithful to the promise until it should be fulfilled, and that he and his family should appreciate the forgiveness for the sin they had brought upon God's good creation.

God looked with favor on Abel and his offering.

The *issue* of that little worship service was a *beginning.*

Abel had come to it with faith in God's promises.

Soon faithful Abel will be martyred because of it.

He will be the first of the saints to walk the streets of glory and to behold the radiant face of God.

His name would head the list of the faithful in the hall of fame, when it should be established, many generations later.

He would be numbered with the greats of the church, not because he was himself great among men, but because he held the faith with them.

Cain left the holy place that day disgruntled.

His chagrin became anger.

His anger smoldered into hatred.

His hatred led to murder.

"Let us go into the open country," he invited his brother.

There, in the open country, with malice aforethought, as we say today, he murdered Abel.

Sin poured indeed through the sluice gate opened in the Fall.

Nor has its raging ceased in all the years since.

"Anyone can see the kind of behavior that belongs to the lower nature: fornication, impurity, and indecency; idolatry and sorcery; quarrels, a contentious temper, envy, fits of rage, selfish ambitions, dissensions, party intrigues, and jealousies; drinking bouts, orgies, and the like" (Galatians 5:19-20 NEB).

The sin of Adam flowed through his sons. Cain let it flow without check He has become a metaphor for anger, and hatred, and murder.

As quietly as God allowed His Son to be born in a stable, just so quietly Abel laid a lamb on an altar outside Eden.

The lamb seems so insignificant in the story. You can miss it altogether if you don't watch for it.

The listener's attention is drawn rapidly away from the *content* of the sacrifices to the people who offered them.

The story seems more the story of Cain, who holds center stage (as far as people go).

Abel holds that place for three or four sentences.

Neither of them will be mentioned again in all the Old Testament, and only in fleeting notice in the New.

But the lamb will play an ever-increasing role.

It is there at the beginning of man's history just outside the angel-guarded gates.

It will be in full focus on the closing pages of Scripture in the stunning climax of St. John's vision.

This is the genesis of the lamb, placed so quietly by the Lord of the promise on the altar where man's first recorded worship service took place.

God used "types" throughout Old Testament history to foreshadow the Christ, who was to come.

Thus the brazen serpent of Moses, which stayed the course of the poison of the asps, was a "type" of Jesus, who frees those who look on Him in faith from the burden of their sins.

And Jonah, three days in the belly of a fish, is a type of the Christ, who was in the bowels of the earth three days until His resurrection.

So the lamb is a type of Jesus.

Again and again God sets a lamb into the history of His people as a type of the Christ.

There came that day when John the Baptist cried out at the appearance of Jesus at the Jordan where he was preaching, "Behold the Lamb of God that takes away the sin of the world."

There came that fate-filled night when the lamb of the Passover was placed on the table in the Upper Room—set before the Lamb of God, type meeting antitype, shadow meeting substance, the promise meeting the fulfillment.

And then, for Abel, for Cain, for Caiphas and the centurion, for you and me, the hours on the cross, when "Christ our Passover was sacrificed for us."

Even now we are under the dominion of the Lamb who was slain, for He is given rule by the Father over all creation.

And at the end we will be, if by grace we are still in the faith, a part of the great supper of the Lamb, and guests at the marriage of the Lamb.

As silently as the type appears, as quietly as Christ became incarnate, so quietly Christ comes to us still.

In the silent waters of Baptism He comes.

In the Word, He comes.

In the holy Sacrament of the Altar, He comes.

He comes to the lonely and despairing.

He comes to the sin-sick and the lost.

He comes to the burden bearer and the frightened.

But we must let Him come—with hearts open to the faith—with repentance and hope—

Through Him we bring our offering to our God.

We leave our sheaves of grain and fruit, our kindly deeds and generous acts, behind us.

We bring only the lamb, only our Lamb, to offer in faith, our sacrifice on our altar.

For, in the end, it is only Christ, the Lamb of God, which causes our heavenly Father to receive us with favor.

2. On the Mountain, the Lamb

Suggested hymns

    O dearest Jesus, what law hast Thou broken

    Lamb of God, pure and holy

    There is a fountain filled with blood

    Now rest beneath night's shadow

Suggested Scripture
    Matthew 26:36-46
    Genesis 22:1-14
    The interwoven Passion story

Suggested Psalm
    Psalm 46

Behold the Lamb

A Litany

(Litany: a resonant or repetitive recital or chant)

Christ our Passover is sacrificed for us.
    Behold the Lamb of God that taketh away the sin of the world.
Abel brought the firstling of his flock.
    Behold the Lamb of God that taketh away the sin of the world.
Abraham lifted his eyes and looked and beheld behind him a ram caught
in the thicket by its horns.
    Behold the Lamb of God that taketh away the sin of the world.
Draw out and take you a lamb, according to your families and kill the
passover.
    Behold the Lamb of God that taketh away the sin of the world.
And Aaron lay both hands upon the head of the live goat, and confessed
over him all the sins of the children of Israel . . . and sent him away by the
hand of a fit man into the wilderness.
    Behold the Lamb of God that taketh away the sin of the world.
He is brought as a lamb to the slaughter, and as a sheep before his shearers
is dumb, so He openeth not His mouth.
    Behold the Lamb of God that taketh away the sin of the world.
The next day John seeth Jesus coming unto him, and saith:
    Behold! The Lamb of God that taketh away the sin of the world.
Now about the sixth hour there was darkness over all the land until the
ninth hour. And about the ninth hour Jesus cried with a loud voice,
saying *"Eli, Eli, lema sabachthani?"*
    Christ our Passover is sacrificed for us.
Ye were not redeemed with corruptible things as silver and gold . . . but
with the precious blood of Christ, as of a lamb without blemish and
without spot.
    Christ our Passover is sacrificed for us.
And the city (heaven) had no need of the sun, neither the moon, to shine
in it; for the glory of God did lighten it, and the Lamb was the light
thereof.
    Behold! The Lamb of God that taketh away the sin of the world.

Singing (All): Glory be to the Father and to the Son and to the Holy Ghost; as it was in the beginning, is now, and ever shall be, world without end. Amen.

On the Mountain, the Lamb

Genesis 22:1-14

Dear Friends of Christ,

In Eden, in the shade of the tree of the knowledge of good and evil, almighty God cursed the seducing Satan.

"I will make you and the Seed of the woman enemies. You will bruise His heel, but He will crush your head."

Satan had reason to tremble. From that moment on, his days of walking to and fro upon the earth were numbered.

The woman and the man had reason to hope.

Eve, the promise of the Seed strong in her memory, beheld Cain and marveled. "I have received a man, the Lord," she whispered.

But Cain was not the Promised One.

Generations would come and go. Seth, Enoch, Methuselah, Noah, Heber, Terah—carried the Seed.

On a starbright night Abraham received the news from God that he carried the Seed in him.

It would be through him that all the nations of the earth should be blessed.

So there had been plan in the move out of Ur of the Chaldees.

There was purpose in the command to leave Padan-Aram to journey to the new land.

God was preparing the world to fulfill His ancient promise.

Abraham, carrier of the Seed, was integral to it.

The years were rolling on.

Sarah, the wife of Abraham's bosom, bore him no children.

It was Sarah who encouraged Abraham to father an offspring by Hagar, her Egyptian maidservant.

A child was born to Hagar.

Abraham was reassured. The possibility of the Seed from his loins was a reality. He had fathered a son, but it was not the son of the promise.

Still the years passed.

Abraham neared 100 years of age.

The promise of God hung in the balance.

Surely it was too late, too late.

But the Lord spoke to Abraham again.

Once more he promised the child, through whom the Seed should be passed on.

The whole ideas was preposterous. He was 99; Sarah was 90, their time of fertility had faded.

But nothing is too hard for the Lord.

Sarah conceived.

They named the child Isaac, which means "laughter," for Sarah's joy was full beyond containing, and Abraham's heart brimmed with gratitude.

Were Isaac not the Promised One, at least the Seed would pass through yet another generation.

The promise made so long ago in the garden was vindicated.

Laugh, all you people. God has kept his promise. God is good.

Laugh, you nations yet to come, for lo, the promised Seed is still among us.

And Sarah and Abraham laughed as the child grew . . . at his first tentative steps . . . at the little funny things he said . . . as he developed into manhood.

They laughed more often at the wonder of God who made and kept His promises, for through their only son, the son of promise, the son of their old age, God had indeed kept the promise alive *another time*.

Then came the testing time.

God came to Abraham with an awesome request.

"Take now thy son, thine only son Isaac, whom thou lovest, into the land of Moriah; and offer him there for a burnt offering upon one of the mountains that I will tell thee of."

The God of promises became the God of the dreadful command.

The God of the First Commandment of the Decalog demanded choice.

Choose, Abraham!

"Me or Isaac."

O fateful day!

But Abraham had made his choice long ago.

He would serve the living God.

The next morning he slipped from his bed without arousing Sarah.

He woke Isaac gently.

He beckoned him to silence, and together they tiptoed out of the tent.

While Isaac fettered the donkey, Abraham gathered wood.

They tied the wood to the donkey's girdle.

Just as the sun was fully over the distant hills, they started in the direction of Moriah.

No word is recorded of the conversations on the three-day journey.

Isaac wondered at his father's silence. He contented himself with his father's taciturn answers to his questions. Even in his youth, he was aware of the distant haunting look in his father's deep, dark eyes.

Abraham had his own deep searching to do.

"Where have I offended God?" he wondered as he searched his life, his soul, for answers.

"He demands of me a burnt offering, the offering for sin."

"What have I not done to please God?"

Each day of the journey came and went. Each day was long beyond measuring.

Yet not once did Abraham, the man of faith and obedience turn to look back, not once did he falter in his journey to Moriah.

At the foot of Moriah they tied the donkey to a long tether.

Abraham bid the lad carry the wood for the sacrifice.

"Where is our lamb?" asked Isaac. He had not yet been told the awesome fact that would require his life this day.

"God will provide." Abraham answered him softly.

Gently, firmly, Abraham bound his son after the manner of binding sacrificial animals.

Isaac offered no resistance, spoke no word, obedient through it all.

And Abraham, if he couldn't understand about the promise of the Seed, he wouldn't argue with God as once he had argued over the fate of Sodom.

He knew as he raised the knife to take Isaac's life that the promise would seem to come to an end.

There was no other through whom the Seed passed to him by his fathers would be passed to coming generations.

He would not bargain with God.

Others have posed hypotheses, "What if's," of the outcome if Abraham had not been quite so obedient, quite so committed to his Lord.

What if Abraham had denied his Lord for the sake of Isaac's peace, saying the sacrifice was his own idea? After all, it is better Isaac should believe Abraham a monster than that he lose his faith in Abraham's God. Would Abraham then ever forgive himself?

"What if" Abraham, seeing the ram, had made the substitution on his own? Ah, then Abraham would suddenly become old, and the laughter he once knew would never happen again.

"What if" Abraham had thought it *sin* to offer his beloved son, a seduction of Satan? Then he would live out his days in doubt, for he would have failed the testing.

Or "what if" Isaac saw, as Abraham raised his hand for the sacrifice, that hand tremble, hesitate for the slightest second. It would have been enough, in that fate-filled moment, for Isaac to lose his faith.

But there are no "what if's" remotely suggested in the story.
Aware of all the fragmentation of hope, all the impending loneliness without his son, Abraham raised his knife for the fatal plunge.

"Abraham. Abraham."
An angel, at that precarious moment, intervened.
"Lay not your hand upon the lad!"

The testing time was over. Abraham had been faithful to the end!
As a prima ballerina leaps through the air to land in perfect poise and balance, on her toes, so Abraham stands in perfect balance in obedience and faith.
As a ship in contrary winds and beating waves, holds steady to its course, so Abraham kept his faith steady toward God.

The angel pointed to a ram caught in the tangled brambles on a hilltop.
Together Abraham and Isaac freed it from the thorny branches that held it steady.
They bound it after the way of binding animals to the sacrifice. And that day they offered *it* to God.
And I think they sang and danced together before the altar.
And they thanked God, and they praised God . . .
And a strong faith was made stronger and a growing faith grew mightily.
And as the worship time came to end, Abraham named the place Jehovah-Jireh, which means "God will provide."
Had not God provided, indeed, for their moment of dread!
Did *He* not net the ram in the underbrush, a substitute sacrifice in that dread-filled moment!

As unobtrusively as a gentle breeze, as subtly as the growth of a flower, God set a lamb (a ram) into the fountainhead, into the stream of the history of His people.
Abraham is the father of all who are faithful to God, first of the Jewish tradition, then of the Christian tradition as well.
As often as the story of Abraham has been told . . . around campfires, in classes, in synagogs and churches, the faithfulness of Abraham has never been missed . . . or the lamb ever failed to have been noticed.
The lamb, provided by Jehovah, as a substitute sacrifice!
Is the distance too far from Abraham's lamb to the other Lamb provided by the same God in the bramble bushes of Calvary?

I think not.

One is shadow, the other is substance.

One is type, the other is antitype.

As St. Paul put it, the bramble-snared lamb is a shadow of things to come, but the shadow-producing body is the cross-entangled Jesus.

Beneath the lessons of Abraham's perfect obedience and faith lies the lesson of the Lamb.

Let no man fail to know God in His sin-hating justice, for it is deception and wishful thinking to know God only as love.

The same word that called the world into existence, pronounced its doom in the death-dealing floodwaters.

The same hands that formed man from the dust, gave the signal to confuse the arrogant people of Babel.

The same heart that would free the Goshen slaves of Egpyt, also required the firstborn of each Egyptian household.

The same great pressures that hardened a Pharaoh's heart, that drove the nations to depravity, or that made hearts ready to exclude God are abroad today.

The *world* is with us too much . . . we can barely escape its octopusian arms. Owning things for the owning's sake, the world owes me a living, self-interest at all costs, pleasure to the exclusion of all else . . . the philosophy of the world without God bends its pressures on us; rare is the youth, the adult, who can withstand them.

Satan has become more adept than ever at creating doubts, to offering rationalizations seducing men into sin and despair and other great shame and vice.

Nor has the *flesh* of man changed. The same internal pressures that drove the citizens of Sodom and Gomorrah into darkness, the same internal voices that urged to self-gratification in Rome, are still at hand.

The man, the woman, who comes to himself/herself somewhere in the pigsty, comes face to face with the righteous God.

Appease the gods, man cries. He offers his firstborn to Molech. He buries his human sacrifices in the foundations of his houses and the city wall.

The silence of his gods is appalling.

He faces two courses.

He can bury God . . . but then he dies to meet an angry God in death . . . and dies again.

He moves to despair . . . and dies broken on wheels of his own devising . . . only to meet the God of justice and die again.

No one is free from the terrifying dilemma; there is no escape.

"God has concluded all under sin."

"There is not a just man upon earth that doeth good and sinneth not."

"The wages of sin is death."

Is not God faithful to his threat of judgment?

Are we not Isaacs, doomed by the righteousness of God?

Do not pursue the thought.

A ram is caught in the brambles; a substitute has been found.

The Son of God has become entangled in the terrible arms of the cross; a substitute has been offered.

Lay hold of that Lamb and set Him on your altar before God.

Let Him carry your sins to death and hell.

Let Satan laugh: "The Seed of promise dies this day; and the ancient prophecy does not hold. I have killed the Prince of Life."

The Lamb bound by nails is offered, God's offering to God, the Son's offering to the Father.

And by it our sins are expiated; by it we are free. God is love. The gift of God is eternal life to all who know and believe the substitution.

Father Abraham, that man of unshakable faith and trust in the righteousness of God, stands preeminent in the "Hall of Fame."

"By faith Abraham, when he was called to go out into a place which he should after receive for an inheritance, obeyed. . . ."

By faith he sojourned in the land of promise. . . .

By faith Abraham, when he was tried, offered up Isaac; and he that had received the promises offered up his only begotten son, of whom it was said, that "in Isaac shall thy seed be called."

He stands at the beginning of the history of God's people.

And with him stands the sure knowledge that God would provide, Jehovah-Jireh.

Ten thousand times ten thousand times the story was told, and always the lamb in the brambles was told with it.

Those who heard the story saw the shadow of things to come.

But we, we have seen the Lamb, the body, the Christ.

He is become our sin-offering.

As often as the story of God's great love is told, the Lamb is in the midst of it.

Jehovah-Jireh, as a pillar of stones, may one day be found by enterprising archaeologists.

The Jehovah-Jireh of the cross—the "God will provide" of the high altar at Calvary—has never been lost.

We have a journey to make.

It starts at the place where God provided that other Lamb, His only begotten Son.

The destination is the mansions, the Jehovah-Jireh of the new promise.
The way is walked by faith and obedience.
The sacrifice is behind us.
"But now they desire a new country, that is, an heavenly: Wherefore God
     is not ashamed to be called their God: for He hath prepared for them
     a city."
Come, good friends in Christ the Lamb, let us lock hands as we journey to
     that better country.

3. In Egypt, the Lamb

Suggested Hymns
     Savior, when in dust to Thee
     O Christ, Thou Lamb of God
     When I survey the wondrous cross
     Sun of my soul, Thou Savior dear

Suggested Scripture
     Matthew 26:57-68
     Exodus 12:1-36
     The interwoven Passion story

Suggested Psalm
     Psalm 23

The Good Shepherd

A Responsive Reading

(Isaiah 53 and Psalm 23)

O come, let us worship and bow down,
     let us kneel before the Lord our Maker.
For He is our God,
     and we are the people of His pasture and the sheep of His hand.
The Lord is my Shepherd,
     I shall not want.
He maketh me to lie down in green pastures.
     He leadeth me beside the still waters.
I have gone astray, like a lost sheep.
     All we like sheep have gone astray.
We are counted as sheep for the slaughter.
     The Shepherd seeks those who have gone astray.
Jesus is the Good Shepherd.
     The Good Shepherd giveth His life for the sheep.
We have turned every one to his own way,
     and the Lord hath laid on Him the iniquity of us all.

He was oppressed and He was afflicted,
> yet He opened not His mouth.
He is brought as a lamb to the slaughter,
> and as a sheep before her shearers is dumb, so He openeth not His mouth.
He was cut off from the land of the living;
> for the transgressions of My people was He stricken.
Christ our Passover is sacrificed for us.
> The Good Shepherd giveth His life for the sheep.
Yea, though I walk through the valley of the shadow of death
> I will fear no evil.
For Thou art with me;
> Thy rod and Thy staff, they comfort me.
Surely goodness and mercy shall follow me all the days of my life;
> and I will dwell in the house of the Lord forever.
Singing (All): Glory be to the Father and to the Son and to the Holy Ghost; as it was in the beginning, is now, and ever shall be, world without end. Amen.

In Egypt, the Lamb

Text: Exodus 12:5-7 (1-28)

Dear Friends of Christ,
We must go back to the Egypt of Moses.
By the time Moses arrived on the stage of history, the majestic pyramids had guarded the land for a thousand years.
The great sphinx had watched the mighty Nile flood and recede for a millennium.
The magnificent temples, edifices for the gods of Egypt, with their hundred-foot columns and endless inscriptions, dominated the cities.
In their graves, the Pharaohs lay in silent splendor amid the wealth of the nation sealed with them in their tombs.
The Hyksos nation had been driven from the land.
For three and a half centuries Pharaohs had maintained their dynasty.

Commerce flourished. The arts flourished. The army was strong. Egypt was feared and admired.
The Nile was then as now the strength of Egypt. Every year that great river flooded, watering the land a short distance on either side, enough to produce the grains and fruits the nation needed.
Beyond that narrow, fertile strip of water and greenery, lay the desert.
Only the life-sustaining waters of the Nile kept the land alive.

It was because of the constant Nile that Joseph and his brothers came to Egypt.

Famine in their own land drove them, along with many of their countrymen, to seek food in this ancient "breadbasket of the world."

The family stayed on in Egypt, settling in the delta lands of the great river known as Goshen.

The family grew through the years into sizable numbers. It was content to farm the delta soil or to find employment in the capitol nearby.

Four hundred years pass, and with the passing years, new Pharaohs.

Joseph's great contribution to Egyptian history was forgotten, and with him the passing history of the people in the delta country.

Pharaohs, unsympathetic to the descendants of Joseph, requisitioned the delta people for building programs in the city.

The descendants of the proud family became slaves in the land that they had espoused.

Of those people, Moses was born. In spite of Pharaoh's edict that all male babies should be slain, Moses and many others survived.

Moses was adopted into the Pharaoh's family by the Pharaoh's daughter.

For 40 years he enjoyed the education, the privileges of the palace.

Then, learning of his "roots," he identified with the slaves, who labored under the blistering Egyptian sun and the stinging whips of their overseers.

In a rage, one day, he attacked and killed a slave driver.

The attack forced his flight into the great desert.

'Here for 40 years he shepherded sheep, leading them wherever he might find water and forage for them.

As he had learned to know Egypt, so now he learned the ways of the nomad in the land of Midian.

When he was 80, though he didn't know it, he was ready for the purpose God had in store for him.

God came to Moses at the burning bush.

"I have seen the affliction of My people which are in Egypt, and have heard their cry by reason of the taskmasters; for I know their sorrows. ... Come now therefore, and I will send thee unto Pharaoh, that thou mayest bring forth My people the children of Israel out of Egypt" (Ex. 3:7-10).

God's hour to gather Himself a people had come.

Moses' education for the task was over.

Now followed the deep encounter with the Pharaoh.

31

No way would he release the slaves.

God plagued Egypt with lice and darkness and a river of blood and other plagues.

Pharaoh vacillated and refused, vacillated and refused, vacillated and refused to let God's people go.

Then the night of terror and freedom!

God would destroy the eldest child in every household and the firstborn of all the beasts.

The visitation would be so horrible that Pharaoh would vacillate no more.

Preparations must be made by the people of Goshen, by the children of God.

Among other things they were to select a lamb.

God's lamb is there again!

It was on the altar at the first recorded worship service.

It was tangled in the bramble bushes at the sacrificial altar on Mount Moriah, where Abraham had been commanded to sacrifice his only son.

Here it is again—in the confusion of the plagues, in the bewilderment of God's people—a sign of their freedom.

Moses delivered the will and plan of God to the people.

Lambs were selected according to instructions.

Small families joined other small families for the meal.

The lamb was slain. It's blood was smeared on each house, one tradition says in the shape of a *tau* (a T-shaped cross).

While the lamb roasted before the fires, the people gathered whatever they could carry.

They dressed for the journey.

While they ate, the Lord required the firstborn of all Egypt in houses that had not been marked with a lamb's blood.

Then the signal!

The march to freedom began.

The slaves of Egypt became the people of God. The holy nation was in the making; God had chosen Himself a people.

But more than that.

The lamb had been placed front and center again on the stage of the history of the people of God when their freedom began.

Conditions permitting, it would be there in the commemoration of the night of the Passover until the time of Christ.

God had given His people a sign. This time not a sign to appear alone in the retelling of the story of Cain and Abel, or of Abraham and Isaac, but a lamb which all the people of God would see and touch and taste at the Passover celebration.
The type anticipating the Antitype . . .
The shadow announcing the Substance . . .
The lamb prophetic of *the* Lamb.

The celebration of the Passover came and went some two thousand times.
Year after year the people of the old Covenant gathered and ate the lamb, and remembered the night freedom came to them.
Each time they celebrated, knowingly or unknowingly, they anticipated another night when *the* Lamb would gather His twelve men about Him to eat the Passover with them.
That night came in God's good time.

Jesus, knowing the hour was at hand, set the hour and the place for the gathering of His disciples.
He was indeed front and center that night.
He talked of many things, almost without stopping . . . of faithfulness and friendship.
It was the night He stooped to wash the dusty feet of all His friends, of Peter and Judas.
That was the night He prayed, oblivious to them all, the prayer for their safekeeping, while He must be separated from them.
He prayed that they all might be one, as He and the Father were one.
They gathered around the table to eat the Passover meal.
The bitter herbs were there, and the unleavened bread, the goblets of wine, called for in the ritual meal.

Together they ate the herbs; together they drank their cups of wine.
The cups had come to reflect the great promises of God.
The first: "I will bring out!"
The second: "I will deliver you from bondage."
The third: "I will redeem you."
And the fourth, "I will take you for My people."
Perhaps it was as they were about to drink the third cup of wine that Jesus paused.
The rehearsal was over.
Two thousand times the rehearsal had gone as scheduled.
The prolog to the drama had begun.

The new Paschal Lamb was identified.
God had chosen *His* Lamb.

The Lamb would this day be led as a sheep to the slaughter.
He would be sacrificed on the rocky altar of the skull-shaped hill.
He would be "spitted" on the cross.
He would be exposed to the raging fires of hell.

His blood, pressured from His brow in Gethsemane, drawn from his hands and feet by nails, and drained from his side by a Roman spear, would be shed.
Not a bone of Him would be broken.
At the same hour that lambs were being sacrificed in the temple, God's Lamb would be dying on the cross.
Christ our Passover would be sacrificed for us.
Now anyone who in faith daubed *the Lamb's* blood (as it were) on the tentpole of his heart would have freedom from God's angel of death.
Everything is the same; everything is different.
God saw the plight of the slaves of Goshen; He saw with gentle compassion the plight of the slaves of the flesh, the slaves of Satan, and the slaves of this world.
As He set the lamb in the midst of the ancient Passover, so He has set His Lamb in the midst of His church.
As they once ate the Passover meal, so God's people today eat the "Passover" of His broken body and spilled blood.
As long ago He led His people to freedom from the tyranny of man, so today He leads His people to freedom from the tyranny of the Law and sin, from His judgment and death.
As once He commanded His people to commemorate the fateful night in Egypt, so we are bid with our Redeemer's words "This do in remembrance of Me" to commemorate His fateful night.
The Passover meal with its prescribed ritual has become the Passover meal of the new covenant, sealed with the body and blood of the Lamb.

The poets have a way of saying things. Richard Massie translated Luther's *Nun freut euch* like this:

> Fast bound in Satan's chains I lay,
> Death brooded darkly o'er me,
> Sin was my torment night and day,
> In sin my mother bore me,
> Yea, deep and deeper still I fell,
> Life had become a living hell,
> So firmly sin possessed me.

It was the last meal of Jesus, on the night before His passion.
It marked the beginning of the new Israel, the people of the new covenant, and freedom!

It has become the great and mystic meal of the Christian church.

At the end of it is freedom; for Christ said once long ago, "If the *Son* therefore shall make you free, ye shall be free indeed" (John 8:36).

Little Passover lamb, symbol of an ancient liberation; you are but the type of that other Passover Lamb, whose blood has set us free to be the people of God.

4. In the Wilderness, the Lamb

Suggested Hymns
>Upon the cross extended
>Come to Calvary's holy mountain
>Not all the blood of beasts
>All praise to Thee, my God, this night

Suggested Scripture
>Matthew 27:11-26
>Leviticus 16
>Hebrews 9:23-28
>The interwoven Passion history

Suggested Psalm
>Psalm 130

Jesus, My Friend

A Responsive Reading

O Lord, our eternity with You is forfeit
and our time knows no peace,
for we stand as sinners before You,
but You have made a way of escape.
>I lay my sins on Jesus,
>The spotless Lamb of God;
We are as unclean things
and all our righteousness is as a filthy rag.
>He bears them all and frees us
>From the accursed load.
There is not one just among us.
Our wages are paid out in death.
>I bring my guilt to Jesus
>To wash my crimson stains
Our souls are dark with sinning
and our sin crouches at our door.

Clean in His blood most precious
Till not a spot remains.

We are beset by illness on the right and the left.
We are burdened with burdens hard to bear.
    I lay my wants on Jesus
    All fullness dwells in Him;
We live in the shadow of sickness;
We know not the number of our days.
    He healeth my diseases,
    He doth my soul redeem.
Sorrow ofttimes encompasses us;
We weep in the nighttime for our loved ones lost.
    I lay my griefs on Jesus
    My burdens and my cares;
We long for surcease from our worrying,
and an end to our nighttime tears.
    He from them all releases,
    He all my sorrow shares.

There is no peace in the world;
The philosophies of men lead but to despair.
    I rest my soul on Jesus,
    This weary soul of mine;
We are lonely in the midst of people,
We long for love, for the touch of a good friend.
    His right hand me embraces,
    I on His breast recline.
Lord, You have given up Your only begotten Son
You have made the name of Jesus great among us.
    I love the name of Jesus,
    Immanuel, Christ, the Lord;
You have sent forth Your gracious Word;
Let men who make the multitudes speak of Your love.
    Like fragrance on the breezes
    His name abroad is poured.

Lord, You have set Your Son for an example;
You have made Him a pattern to follow.
    I long to be like Jesus,
    Meek, loving, lowly, mild;
You have adopted us into Your holy family;
You have made us siblings of the Christ.

I long to be like Jesus,
The Father's holy Child.
Hold us in Your love, stay by us in time,
Maintain us in the faith, and keep us in Christ.
I long to be with Jesus
Amid the heavenly throng.
For we would join the celestial choirs
And sing Your praise with the saints in glory.
To sing with saints His praises,
To learn the angels' song.

In the Wilderness, the Lamb

Text: Leviticus 16:1-10; Hebrews 9:23-28

Dear Friends of Christ,

Yom Kippur, the Day of Atonement, ofttimes referred to as *The Day,* was instituted by God in the days of Moses, when Aaron was high priest of the tabernacle.

God prescribed certain rites for it.

In quick outline, the rites and rituals of the day went as follows:

Aaron was to choose a young bull for a sin offering and two goats for sin and whole offerings.

After grooming himself, he was to offer the bull as an expiation for himself and his family. One goat was offered for the people. With a pitcher of the blood of the animals, and two handfuls of incense, he then entered (it must have been with great awe and much trembling) the Holy of Holies, the most sacred place in all the land. God, you see, dwelt in the Holy of Holies in all His majesty and mystery.

Aaron sprinkled the sacrificial blood on the ark of the covenant. He mixed the blood of the bull with the blood of one of the goats. As he walked about the great altar seven times, he sprinkled the blood on it to expiate the people's sins.

In the Tent of the Presence before the assembled people, a second rite took place. The other goat was brought to him. With great ceremony he solemnly placed both hands on the head of the little animal as he made confession of all the people's sins and rebellious acts against the Lord. The sin of the people was thus transferred to the hapless goat.

With appropriate gestures, Aaron signaled the man appointed to the task to lead the goat, laden with its sin, out into the wilderness. The name of the place to which the goat was taken was called Azazel (the name is also applied to the goat and to Satan).

The great, solemn, moving service was over.

Aaron and his family were absolved.

The sin of the nation had been carried into the wilderness by Azazel, the "scapegoat."

"God is good," the people cried, and a rousing celebration began.

Once again the Lamb motif is introduced into history and the Scriptures.

The motif has been recurring since the lamb offering of Abel was accepted by God in the beginning of history outside the Garden of Eden.

On Moriah the lamb, substituted for Isaac in that fearful demand of God on Abraham to offer his beloved son, anticipated the vicarious satisfaction of Jesus, Lamb of God.

In the last day in Egypt, the Passover lamb was set into history as a type of the great Paschal Lamb, who should bring freedom from sin and death.

Now, in the midst of the wilderness wanderings, two lambs, one whose blood was sprinkled in the Holy of Holies and one who bore sin into the wilderness, are introduced into the continuing ritual of God's Old Testament people. Both have become shadows of that other Lamb, whose blood was shed for the sin of the world and who bore the sin of the world in His own body on the accursed tree of the cross.

The lamb led to the precipice bearing the people's guilt was the original scapegoat. On it the people placed their sins for which they were accountable. Through it the people found release and relief from their guilt and accountability.

The scapegoat is a person or a thing bearing the guilt of others. The Christians were scapegoats for Nero at the burning of Rome. The Jews were scapegoats for Hitler as he sought to cleanse the German nation of its non-Aryan blood to create a superrace. One's little sister is blamed for the slamming screen door.

Christ is our Azazel, our scapegoat. The sin of the world was placed on Him. He was expunged from the church, the nation, from all humanity. He died for the sin of the world in the wilderness of Calvary.

The poets haven't missed the scapegoat Christ. Horatius Bonar, 1843, penned the beloved hymn

> I lay my sins on Jesus,
> The spotless Lamb of God:
> He bears them all and frees us
> From the accursed load.

And Isaac Watts, probably the greatest of the hymnists, wrote:

> My faith would lay her hand
> On that dear head of Thine
> While like a penitent I stand
> And there confess my sin.

Once a year, year after year, the scapegoat symbolically bore the sins of the nation into the darkness.

Once Christ took into Himself the sins of the world, and through all the years since, God's people in faith have known the forgiveness of their sins accomplished when He went into the wilderness of the cross and our hell.

Once for all time.

Once for all people.

Two goats on the Day of Atonement, one the scapegoat, the other an expiation for the sin of the people as well. The significance of the second goat overshadows that of the first.

The second goat was slain according to the accustomed ceremonial ritual.

It's blood was caught in a proper vessel.

Aaron (and those who followed him in the office) carried it into the Holy of Holies to sprinkle it on the appurtenances in the holy place for the people's uncleanness and acts of rebellion against God. Thus the expiation was made for the people. So atonement was accomplished in the framework of the old covenant.

Strictly speaking, the atonement was not the preparation and the sacrifice of the animal so much as the *official* presentation of the blood of the animals to the Lord in that space behind the veil where God Himself was present.

The implications of the atonement, under the concern of the Holy Spirit, came into sharp focus in the New Testament book of the Hebrews.

Hebrews is an attempt to gather the theology and the practices, the sacrifices and prophecies, the hopes and promises of the Old Testament people and in telling point after point to apply them to Jesus, who is the Christ.

If the angels had authority in history, the Son of God has authority now.

If Moses was a faithful servant, Christ is a faithful Son.

If Melchizedek was a type of Christ, Christ is the antitype.

The Levitical priesthood was important; it has been exceeded by the new High Priest, Christ.

The old God-given ceremonial practices were but symbols until Christ came.

Christ makes the old order obsolete and Himself makes the perfect sacrifice.

As the high priest entered the Holy of Holies to make atonement, so Christ has entered heaven to make atonement for us.

Hebrews was written for people of the Jewish persuasion; it is packed with insights and excitement for all Christians.

Consider the Christ.

He was the sheep chosen for the slaughter.

He was holy, harmless, undefiled.

He refused to use His divine powers to change the nefarious course of His trial and execution.

He took upon Himself the sin of the world, scapegoat for the whole human family.

He took upon Himself the whole wrath of a just God against sin.

He endured the terrors of hell in the dark hours of that terrible day of the Lord.

He suffered the Satanic celebration in His high-noon commitment.

When at last the ransom for the soul of man had been paid, He announced His victory in His cry from the cross, "It is finished!"

Like the sacrificial lamb on the Day of Atonement, He died for the sin of the world.

Christ's crucifixion and death fill the words of the faith like redemption and ransom and reconciliation and atonement with deep meaning.

Now, we are speaking of the atonement.

We have said that the atonement (in the Old Testament practices) was the precise act of sprinkling the blood of the sacrifice for sin before the Lord in the Holy of Holies.

The Atonement, in Hebrews, in its strictest and best sense, is the presentation of His own blood at the throne of God in heaven by Christ, our High Priest.

Christ, our High Priest, substantivized the atonement of old.

As He ascended into heaven, He entered that for which the Holy of Holies stood. "For Christ is not entered into the holy places made with hands, which are figures of the true, but into heaven itself, now to appear in the presence of God for us" (Hebrews 9:24). Or again, "Who is he that condemneth? It is Christ that died, yea rather, that is risen again, who is even at the right hand of God, who also maketh intercession for us" (Romans 8:34). "If any man sin, we have an advocate [one who pleads cause for another] with the Father, Jesus Christ, the righteous" (1 John 2:1).

Let there be peace and gratitude and joy, yes, and celebration.

It is staggering to me to think that God holds our universe in His hands, or that He knows the movement of the minutest particles of which the stuff of our earth is made.

I can only handle that by calling God's preservation of our universe in all of its vastness and minuteness a divine mystery.

It is equally staggering, given the tens of millions of people who populate our earth at this moment—and all who have gone before or are still to come—that all, at once, are in the divine consciousness. It is a divine mystery.

It is far beyond my grasping that Christ could have died for all the sin of all the world to redeem its tens of millions of souls. It is a divine mystery.

This I know and this I believe, that my heavenly Father knows and loves me . . . that Christ ransomed and reconciled me to my Lord.

And this I know and this I believe, that my High Priest even now is in the heavens, with His blood spilled for me, making intercession for me.

And this I pray and this I believe, that you as the people of God have made covenant with the Christ.

He bore your sin in His own body on the tree . . . into the wilderness of the cross.

He pleads your case, even now, . . . in the Holy of Holies, in heaven.

And this I know, that the sacrifice was made and the atonement is available for all.

The heathen man, whose gods are silent and unhearing, let him come to the Christ and find the living, gracious God. Christ stands ready for him to cry, "O Lamb of God, I come, I come," for He has presented His holy precious blood to the Father for him.

Let the most abject of sinners, the despairing, the dying, come to Him, for He has presented His blood to the Father.

O world! hear the glorious Gospel of redemption and atonement and find in Christ the peace that passes all understanding.

Did you realize, prime high priest of the holy faith, out there in the wilderness tabernacle, as you laid your hands on Azazel, that you were type for the Father who would place the world's sin on His Lamb? Did you know that you were type for the Christ of God who would enter the eternal Holy of Holies, to present His blood at the throne for every sinner?

> Jesus, my great High Priest,
> Offered His blood and died;
> My guilty conscience seeks
> No sacrifice beside.
> His pow'rful blood did once atone,
> And now it pleads before the Throne.

5. In Captivity, the Lamb

Suggested Hymns
>Go to dark Gethsemane
>Throned upon the awful tree
>Rock of Ages, cleft for me
>Abide with me, fast falls the eventide

Suggested Scripture
>Matthew 26:22-31
>Isaiah 53
>The interwoven Passion story

Suggested Psalm
>Psalm 114

As a Lamb

A responsive reading based on Isaiah 53 and Philippians 2

Let this mind be in you which was also in Christ Jesus,
who, being in the form of God,
thought it not robbery to be equal with God—
>Who hath believed our report?
>And to whom is the arm of the Lord revealed?

But made Himself of no reputation—
>He is despised and rejected of men;
>a man of sorrows and acquainted with grief:
>and we hid as it were our faces from Him;
>He was despised, and we esteemed Him not.

And took upon Him the form of a servant—
>Surely He hath borne our griefs and carried our sorrows;
>Yet we did esteem Him stricken, smitten of God, and afflicted.

And was made in the likeness of men—
>But He was wounded for our transgressions,
>He was bruised for our iniquities—

And being found in fashion as a man—
>the chastisement of our peace was upon Him;
>and with His stripes we are healed.

He humbled Himself
and became obedient unto death—
>All we like sheep have gone astray;
>We have turned every one to his own way;
>And the Lord hath laid on Him the iniquity of us all.

Even the death of the cross.
>He was cut off out of the land of the living:
>for the transgressions of My people was He stricken.

Wherefore God also hath highly exalted Him
And given Him a name which is above every name—
>that at the name of Jesus every knee should bow,
>. . . and that every tongue should confess
>that Jesus Christ is Lord,
>to the glory of God the Father.

Singing (All): Glory be to the Father and to the Son and to the Holy Ghost; as it was in the beginning, is now, and ever shall be, world without end. Amen.

In Captivity, the Lamb

Text: Isaiah 53:7

Dear Friends of Christ,

The Moses years and the 40 years of wandering about in the wilderness came to an end together.

The Record says Moses climbed Mount Nebo, saw the Promised Land in the distance, and quietly died.

All Israel wept for him in the lowlands of Moab for 30 days.

Leadership fell to Joshua, the deliverer. The people followed him willingly.

The time for the conquest of the Promised Land had come.

Joshua proved an able leader. Under his leadership assault began on the tribes that held the territory.

Jericho, at the sound of trumpets, fell.

Then, in sweeping thrusts, tribe after tribe was conquered.

When Joshua's days ended, a loose federation of the 12 tribes of Israel dominated the land.

The period of rule by judges ensued.

The judges provided leadership, rising to meet the need of a tribe against an invading enemy, then returning to their daily round.

At the insistence of the people, Samuel anointed Saul king.

Saul had a genius for organization. Under his leadership the tribal federation was welded into a kingdom.

David, shepherd boy, succeeded Saul.
David brought power and prestige to the new nation.
He was a great commander in chief of the army, a most able leader in peace.
In spite of his sinful lapses, he was committed to the God of Israel. His beautiful psalms became the very prayers of Jesus.
At his death, he left a strong, rich, influential kingdom to his son, Solomon.

Solomon, the man of such notable wisdom, brought culture to the nation.
He built the temple on Zion for worship and maintained the stables at Megiddo to defend the nation.
He left behind him a kingdom divided.

The kings of the northern half of the division left the worship of Yahweh. All of them died and "slept with their fathers."
The prophets sent by God—Elijah, Amos, Hosea—called the kings and their subjects back to the Covenant to no avail.
In 721 B.C. Sargon II, an Assyrian king, raided the northern kingdom and carried its people into slavery and oblivion.

In the southern kingdom, the rulers were both evil and good.
God's call to them to faithfulness was issued through mighty prophets like Isaiah, Jeremiah, Ezekiel.
In the end, judgment against them came through the Babylonians.
King Nebuchadnezzar's forces marched in.
They destroyed the temple. Its appurtenances became spoils of war.
Great numbers of the people were taken into exile in Babylonia.

Life in Babylonia was quite tolerable. The exiles were free to purchase property, to establish businesses, to found banks.
But the exile was a judgment of God.
They were people in an alien land.
Their beloved temple was back home and in ruins.
They were people without a country.
Freedom in Babylonia proved a far cry from freedom in their own land.
The longing to go home gnawed at their very cores.

Then, in the midst of their growing homesickness, the voice of the prophet sounded in the land.

His words came to them like a freshening breeze, bringing hope.

"Comfort ye, comfort ye My people, saith your God. Speak ye comfortably to Jerusalem and cry unto her that her warfare is accomplished, that her iniquity is pardoned; for she hath received of the Lord's hand double for all her sins" (Isaiah 40:1).

God had not forgotten them!
Soon, soon, they would be returning home!

Of profound significance in the writing of Isaiah, the prophet of the exile, is the Song of the Servant of Yahweh.
The song occurs in five different stanzas spotted through the prophet's work.
It reaches its great climax in the 53d chapter of Isaiah.
Here in glorious and profound description, in wondrous detail, it pictures the suffering of the Servant of Yahweh.

There can be no doubt that it is of the Christ that the song is speaking, for in detail after detail the poet describes the passion of Jesus.
And in the very center of the stanza the Lamb appears.
The words are so familiar, "He is brought as a lamb to the slaughter ...," so beloved, so profound as to make this verse of the song the heart of the Old Testament.
Of the "lamb" pictures of the Old Testament it is the blossoming of the type into reality.
And it is set into history, once again, as Israel moves into a new phase of her history.
The exiled nation is about to return home.

One almost comes to expect the lamb theme at strategic points.
The first family faces its unknown future as Abel's sacrificial lamb was sacrificed outside Eden.
The bramble-entangled lamb on Mount Moriah, substitute for Isaac, son of the promise, stands at the gateway to Israel's history.
Yahweh God set the Passover lamb among His people while they were still in Egypt, and the scapegoat at the beginning of the development of their ceremonial rites.
The Lamb, in the Song of the Suffering Servant, is as carefully placed at a significant place in Israel's history.
But the lamb theme has taken on new meaning, new purpose, and, above all, an identity.
It has unmistakably become a Person.

The prophet thinks of the human family as a great flock of sheep.

He carefully notes that "All we like sheep have gone astray; we have
  turned every one to his own way" (53:6).
It is, of course, the poet speaking.
The man who likes to define words precisely might have said, "Mankind
  is in rebellion against God."
The theologian says, "There is not a just man upon earth that doeth good
  and sinneth not" (Eccl. 7:20), or, "The Scripture hath concluded all
  under sin" (Gal. 3:22).
But it is no matter. There is no mistaking the poet's meaning.
We, all mankind, are like sheep without a shepherd, scattered willfully
  about the wilderness.
The judgment of God was upon the sheep.
Gone astray, disobedient, they were marked for slaughter.
God's justice and God's judgment are absolute and inevitable.
There is no escape.

But wait, the Lord singles out one Sheep from the flock.
One without blemish or spot.
On that One the Lord lays the iniquity of all the sheep.
He, of all the sheep is singled out for slaughter for all the sheep.
"He is brought as a lamb to the slaughter, and as a sheep before her
  shearers is dumb, so He openeth not His mouth."

How carefully, how magnificently, the poet-prophet makes his point.
How precisely the picture fits our Jesus.
Like the poet's sheep, Jesus identified Himself with us.
There was nothing to set Him apart from any other man.

When He taught in the Nazareth synagog, the congregation wanted to
  murder Him.
When He stilled the stormy sea they wondered, "What manner of man is
  this?"
When He died, they were bewildered.
He identified Himself with our troubles.
In compassion He healed the sick, raised the depressed, and sat at meals
  with sinners.
So complete was the identification that He took "our sins in His own
  body on the tree."
"He was made to be sin for us, He who knew no sin."
How beautifully the poet-prophet makes his point.
"The Lord hath laid on Him—[on Him who identified Himself with
  us]—the iniquity of us all."
In the poet's language the process is described in detail.
What vivid pictures the poet draws with his words!

He has borne our griefs, carried our sorrows, was wounded for our
transgressions, the chastisement of our peace was upon Him.
The great action words build and build against Him, for in passive
obedience
He was brought as a lamb to the slaughter—
He was stricken, He was smitten, He was humbled, He was pierced,
He was crushed.
The poet's insight grasps the enormous fact: it was for "us all"—for "all
we like sheep" had "gone astray."

The Song of the Suffering Servant is the song of the passion of Jesus.
It can be laid like a grid over the accounts of the last days of our Lord.
It was Caiaphas, high priest, who spoke the "of us all."
"It is expedient for one man to die for the people," he said.
One sheep for the flock, one Man for the world.
The process of the Passion is the extermination of one Man; the process of
salvation is through that one Man.
Caiaphas led the tragic progress—all the way to Calvary.
Sure of his ground at the sentencing, he put the question to a vote.
"What think ye?" he cried. "He is guilty of death," clamored the
Sanhedrin.
King Herod joined the death march to Calvary.
He made political jokes as he sent our Jesus back to Pilate.
And Pilate took his place, at the parade's head, with Caiaphas and Herod
as he washed his hands and exclaimed, "See you to it."
Caiaphas moved up front with his response. "His blood be on us and on
our children," he said.
Somewhere just behind them was Simon of Cyrene, who at spear point
carried His cross.
Hard behind him, the carpenter who fashioned the cross, and soldiers
with hammer and nails, and spears.
And all about the hill were the sheep for whom the Sheep was
slaughtered, making faces at Him, laughing at Him, mocking Him.

But hold on a minute. The poet's insights must not be overlooked.
"The Lord hath laid on Him the iniquity of us all," the poet writes.
The Father is in the midst of it all, like a high priest. It is He who, like the
high priest laying his hands on the head of the scapegoat to
symbolize the Sinbearer, now lays His hands upon Christ, with the
sin and sins of all the world.
The Father is laying His judgment born of justice on His Son.
He is driving Him into the wilderness of hell with the sin of us all upon
Him.
It is the Father's will that One should die for the people!

47

"God so loved the world that He gave [up to die] His only begotten Son."
"The Lord has laid on Him the iniquity of us all."
The cry is from the wilderness, the utter aloneness of being forsaken by
the Father, that the terrifying cry sounds in the darkness on
Calvary—"My God, my God, why hast Thou forsaken Me?"
The Sheep, dumb before His shearers, is led to the slaughter.
"For us all."
"For with—His stripes—we—are healed."

There are lessons to be learned from the Song of the Suffering Servant.
Our Savior knew and is indeed the supreme example of love.
In love He identified Himself with sinners, a Sheep among the sheep.
To do us good He would have to be one of us.
"He took upon Him the form of a servant . . . and being found in fashion
as a man He humbled Himself," even unto death.
Love does that kind of thing.
It identifies with people who need love.
The names of giants emerge. Albert Schweitzer, for instance, who might
have taken the intellectual world, or the musical world, by storm,
chose to minister to the hurting and the dying in far-off Africa.
Toyohiko Kagawa, living in a 6'x6' room in the slums of Kobe,
ministered through a lifetime to the outcasts of his city and nation,
though he might well have lived in mansions and moved govern-
ments in position of authority.
The nameless giants are about us. Missionaries, champions of the city's
derelicts, workers among the cities' outcasts—and Louise, who for
months has nursed her bedridden husband singlehandedly; or Carl,
who cannot leave the house for very long for fear his wife will fall
again; or John, who hurried home from work every evening, hoping
he would not find that Peggy had died during the day—to name a
few.
In our commitment to Jesus, can we do less than commit ourselves to each
other . . . and to the endless unlovely and unloved of our community?
Can anyone be helped in his predicament if we are silent and aloof?

Jesus interposed Himself between us and the judgment of the Father.
When we can, as we can, if we can, we ought, as well, to come to the aid of
every brother (or sister) whose life is in jeopardy, and whose
immortal soul is in danger.
Most of us can't be giants, but all of us can stand tall in our commitment
to love our neighbor as ourselves.

Sing on, poet of the exile, sing on until Your song reaches the heart of
every man.

Sing on, to me and my loved ones of the Lamb by whose stripes we are
    healed.
Sing on, until the people of God love enough to stand tall in the loveless
    world.
Sing on, that new giants may walk upon the earth for Jesus.

6. On the Jordan Banks, the Lamb

Suggested Hymns
    Jesus, I will ponder now
    Comfort, comfort ye My people
    Lord Jesus, think on me
    Holy Father, in Thy mercy

Suggested Scripture
    Matthew 26:24-44
    John 1:29-36
    The interwoven Passion story

Suggested Psalm
    Psalm 22

Behold, the Lamb of God

A Litany

(Litany: a resonant or repetitive recital or chant)

'In the mystery of the Godhead in the reaches of eternity—
    Behold, the Lamb of God.
In a manger at Bethlehem one holy night—
    Behold, the Lamb of God.
In the wilderness with the prince of night—
    Behold, the Lamb of God.
On the mountainside and on a storm-tossed sea—
    Behold, the Lamb of God.
In Gethsemane, pressed against the earth—
    Behold, the Lamb of God.
In the sound of whiplash and dripping water—
    Behold, the Lamb of God.
High on a cross atop a hill called Calvary—
    Behold, the Lamb of God.
In the noontime midnight, cut off from the land of the living—
    Behold, the Lamb of God.
In the stillness of death in the Arimathean's grave—

49

Behold, the Lamb of God.
In resurrection splendor on the Galilean shores,
    Behold, the Lamb of God.
In the glory of the heavens amid the hosts of angels—
    Behold, the Lamb of God.
In the hearts and lives of all who worship here today—
    Behold, the Lamb of God.
In the midst of gathered saints assembled—
    Behold, the Lamb of God.
Singing (All): Glory be to the Father and to the Son and to the Holy Ghost; as it was in the beginning, is now, and ever shall be, world without end. Amen.

On the Jordan Banks, the Lamb

Text: John 1:29

Dear Friends of Christ,
While the Israelites were in exile in Babylon, Persia climbed into power.
Cyrus, a benevolent conqueror, did not pillage and destroy the lands he conquered. "No house was plundered, no man was butchered."
The exiles were freed from their bondage, and by royal decree were permitted to return to their native land.
In 537 B.C. a caravan of 42,360 people, also about 7,300 servants and maids; 736 horses; and mules, camels, and asses left Babylon to make the 800-mile pilgrimage home.
Cyrus sent along the temple appurtenances in reparation.
No edict has effected Christian history quite as much as this one, for the fate of Israel and the birth of Christ were in the balance in those 70 years of exile.
The temple, the city, the old homes were in a shambles when the exiles arrived home.
Under terribly adverse conditions they began the rebuilding processes.
Work on the temple was crucial, but what with the poverty and pressing need for homes, the work lagged, dragged, and stopped. Only after 20 years was work on the temple resumed and completed.
For 200 years the Persians were the liege lord of Jersualem.
The period is marked with lassitude. There is nothing to report, save that the people existed; for in the archaeological digs in that strata of history only simple household utensils have been uncovered. Life was poor in Judah.

Then new nations rose to power.
The Macedonian, Alexander the Great, at the age of 24, defeated Darius III, in 333 B.C.

50

The Macedonians were soon to dominate the world.

Alexander conquered Egypt, then besieged and conquered Tyre, and with it Syria and Palestine.

When he conquered Jerusalem, Alexander offered sacrifices in the temple.

Alexander founded the great city and cultural center of Alexandria in the Nile Delta.

The Greek Empire was split into three kingdoms, Macedonia to the north, the Seleucid kingdom through Asia, and the Ptolemaic kingdom from the Nile to Palestine.

In these Greek-dominated years Judaism reached its lowest tides.

The language largely slipped from the people in favor of Greek. Religion as such all but disappeared.

It was at this time that the first translation of the Old Testament was made into Greek at the great library in Alexandria, an absolutely phenomenal work, for no translation had before been made, and work proceeded without dictionaries and other reference works.

Christianity and Judaism are forever indebted to the Greek translation (known as the Septuagint). It was the counterpart of today's modern translations, the Bible in the language of the people.

Now the Old Testament was available and intelligible to people of other tongues and races. The "tents of Shem" were wide open for the first time in history.

The Greek influence in Palestine was considerable.

Greek culture, Greek thought, the Greek language prevailed.

The games of the Greeks became the sport of the Jewish youth . . . to the horror of the faithful.

Greek games were played naked; the circumcised young people were met with scorn, ridicule, and aversion, as they entered contests away from home.

In 168 B.C. the Seleucid king, Antiochus, seized the land, plundered the temple at Jerusalem.

He sent in his tax collectors, then set houses on fire, and took women and children captive.

An altar of Zeus was set up in the temple.

The sacred scrolls of the Holy Scriptures were destroyed.

A thoroughgoing religious persecution began.

The time was soon ripe for revolt.

Mattathias of Modin refused to sacrifice to pagan gods.

When ordered to do so, he slew the king's commissioner and with his five sons fled to the mountains.

In the hills they gathered a band of followers and waged guerilla warfare
against the Seleucid empire.

Gaining force, the guerillas liberated Jerusalem (164 B.C.) and restored
the old ways in the temple.

Under the leadership of the Maccabean brothers, the warfare subdued the
invading Seleucids, brought religious liberty back to the Jews, and in
the end secured political freedom as well.

By incessant and purposeful fighting the boundaries were extended until
at last they reached the borders of old Solomon's kingdom.

In the year 63 B.C., the Roman army under Pompey arrived in Palestine.
Judah became a Roman province.

And Rome became the mistress of the world.

Thus it was that Caesar Augustus issued a proclamation that all the
world should be enrolled, and everyone went to his own city. And
Joseph and Mary also went up to Bethlehem, to be enrolled in the
census.

And so it was that Christ was born in Bethlehem—
when the world and the land were under the will of Rome;
when Greek was the common language;
when the Jews remembered their quiet past and yearned for the
place and peace and freedom they had known.

In due course of time, John the Preparer of the way for Christ, began to
preach and baptize at the Jordan River.

News of this new prophet and his message stirred the people with new
hope.

The crowds who attended him heard his call to repentance with renewed
hope.

Was this a great prophet returned—Moses? Elijah?

Even King Herod made the journey to the river to see this new revivalist.

Time and again the call to repentance and to Baptism was issued. People,
captivated by this preacher, answered the call and stepped into the
river to receive John's baptism.

Then, one day, Jesus appeared in the crowd.

John stopped speaking, his eyes riveted on this new arrival on the scene.

The people waited expectantly for him to continue his discourse.

Then slowly they turned their eyes to see who or what had caused the
interruption.

At last John speaks.

In a single statement he draws all the significance of the sacrificial lambs
of the old covenant systems into his words—and sets the stage for the
mighty acts of God in the new covenant with his words.

"Behold!"—and look with wonder, with awe—
"Behold, the Lamb of God which taketh away the sin of the world."
The Lamb, for which all the other lambs were types, had come at last.
This Jesus is the antitype.
For three years He will live among the lambs of the land.
Three Passovers will come and go and three times the scapegoat will be
    released into the wilderness.
Then this Lamb, without blemish and without spot, will become the
    sacrifice supreme chosen by God for the expiation of the world's sin.
"Behold, the Lamb of God which taketh away the sin of the world!"

St. John the evangelist does not record the effect of the Baptizer's
    announcement to the crowd.
His readers are left to hear the words for themselves and to react to them.
But St. John does tell us that two men heard and grasped at the truth and
    followed Jesus. One of them is identified. He was Andrew, Simon
    Peter's brother.
The evangelist has established the thesis for his gospel.
From now on he will not deviate from this theme that Jesus, the Christ, is
    the very Lamb of God, the Savior of the world.

The tens of thousands of lambs slain on Jewish altars through the long
    years of their waiting were shadows.
On the banks of the Jordan the Substance casting the shadow is
    identified.
Soon, soon, with rending of the temple veil, the shadows will be no more.
    The Lamb of God has been identified.

The whole force of the Good News in Jesus Christ is summed up in
    John's one sentence.
Jesus will take upon Himself the sin of the world.
It is beyond comprehension.
"Sin," here you see, is the great mass of sin.
It is the sum total, the staggering total, of all the sin of all mankind.
As many people as there are in the world, each with his own mass of daily
    sins of his mind and mouth and hands, and his own life's total of
    sins—and all these masses set together in a total supermass—these
    are the sin of the world.
In the judgment of God any one sin is deadly, damning.
Multiply the sin by millions and multiply it again and again.
It has all been laid upon the back of Jesus, who in His death, like the
    scapegoat of old, bore it away to be remembered no more.
Isaiah in his prophetic utterances had anticipated in the same way
    (Isaiah 53):

"God laid on Him the iniquity of us all" (v. 6).

"For the transgression of My people was He stricken" (v. 8).

The old law is a terrible and terrifying taskmaster.

Its frightening "Thou shalt's" and "Thou shalt not's" lead only to damnation, for they are incapable of being kept—or of relief.

The Law opens us to our sins, condemns us for them, but does not remove them.

All the mental gymnastics, all the psychological exercises we might engage in, do not remove sin.

All the good works we do, do not remove sin.

We are left with it to weigh us down, an unrelieved burden.

There are only two places for the burden of sin to rest.

It either stays on us, or God lays it on His Lamb.

There is only one way to find surcease from the burden of sin.

That is in the Lamb of God.

The Lamb, the Christ, in effect, incorporated all people since Adam into Himself.

He became the whole world.

It was the sacrifice that redeemed the world, the whole family of man.

The Book of Hebrews separates the lambs from *the* Lamb, the high priests from *the* High Priest (7:26-27):

"Such an High Priest became us who is holy, harmless, undefiled, separate from sinners, and made higher than the heavens; who needeth not daily, as those high priests, to offer up sacrifice, first for His own sins and then for the people's; for this He did once when He offered up Himself."

In effect God says, "Dear man, dear woman, you cannot bear your own sin and guilt, for the load is more than you can carry. You cannot free yourself from My judgment against your sin. Therefore, behold, I will lay your sins upon My Lamb and relieve you of it. Believe this. If you do, you are delivered of your sins."

"Behold God's Lamb that takes away your sin."

This passage of St. John's Gospel stands with the great verses of the Bible and the faith.

It is so easily read and so easily missed.

It marks the division point between the time of the Law and the time of the Gospel, the old covenant and the new covenant.

It gathers strength and purpose from the past and anticipates the future.

It presents the Good News to us in the simplest yet most profound of words.

"Behold the Lamb of God . . ."

. . . with the knowledge that He must be offered up
. . . misunderstood by the people
. . . tried and excommunicated by His church
. . . outlawed by His nation
. . . expunged from the family of man
. . . negated in the company of thieves
. . . in hell
    . . . stricken.
    . . . smitten of God,
    . . . and afflicted
"Behold the Lamb of God" . . .
. . . risen from the dead
. . . ascended into glory
. . . sitting at the right hand of God
    . . . the Light of heaven
    . . . amid His redeemed saints in glory
    . . . the hope of His redeemed saints in time

Christ is the center of everything!
Cling to the Lamb. Let no man or devil take Him from you.
For by faith you hold your invitation to the Lamb's marriage feast; by
    faith you hold your passport to heaven.

> Lamb of God, pure and sinless
> Once on the cross an offering,
> Patient, meek, though guiltless,
> Forsaken in your suffering!
> You died our guilt to banish
> That none in sin need perish!
> Your peace be with us, O Jesus.

Holy Week

Invitation to the Holy Week Services
at Saint John Doe's

Dear Friends,
When the crocuses and daffodils splay their brilliant colors low upon the
    earth,
and the flowering trees burst into splendor,
and the singing of the birds is heard again . . .
when the last gray snow is gone,
and the sky turns blue,
and the winds gentle and blow warm across the greening grass . . .
know that the time of life has come again,
know that the days of commemoration and celebration
        of our Lord's death in our stead
        and His resurrection as the firstfruits of them that sleep are here.

To effect our redemption
the High Priest chose to become the Sacrifice, the Shepherd chose to be
    the sacrificial Lamb.
With the frightening hill called Golgotha for altar, in the company of
    thieves, like smoking candles to either side,
the Lamb was offered in our stead.

It is of the Lamb we plan to speak
as in this holy season
we worship in profound response
to the vast mystery of our God who is both offered and received
as sacrifice

and who, because He interposed Himself between the judgment and the
    judged,
was raised from the grave at Easter dawn
and even now reigns in splendor as our Lord.

Behold! the Lamb of God that taketh away the sin of the world. Alleluia!

The plan for worship in our community is here enclosed
for posting in your home.
Consider this an announcement of our plans if you are of the
     congregation.
And if you are our friend, it is our invitation
to be our guest and fellow worshiper at the Lamb's high feasts.

In Jerusalem, the Lamb

(Palm Sunday)

Luke 19:37-38

Dear Friends in Christ,
     St. John at the outset of his gospel set his readers to watching the
unfolding of the history of the Christ, with the cry, "Behold the Lamb of
God who takes away the sin of the world." His readers are bid to keep an
open eye, an open ear, and an open heart as his gospel proceeds. In the
hands of the Holy Spirit the Baptist's cry is an invitation to watch, to
meditate, to repent, to believe—for in the word and deeds of Christ the call
to faith is heard. Now, as the story of Jesus moves relentlessly toward His
suffering and death, the Baptist's cry takes on deeper significance, for the
reader is about to be confronted with the awesome story of the crucifixion
of Jesus and the death of God. The events of Palm Sunday usher into view
the crucial hours of Christ's life and confront the heart and mind with the
stuff from which salvation comes.
     The occasion of the triumphal entry of Jesus into Jerusalem
occurred six days before the Passover celebration. That would account for
the arrival of the pilgrims into the Holy City. Some traveled long
distances from other countries to keep the feast in the great city so central
to their culture and their religion. Already many of the people of the
homeland had arrived, and more were coming every day.
     Sheep and lambs were arriving in the city by the thousands. There
must be enough of them for the sacrifices at the temple and for the tables
of the many gatherings of celebrating relatives and friends. Time was
required to shop for a proper animal at a proper price. Already the buying
and the selling was in progress against the weekend celebration.
     Now, behold the Lamb of God! He might have come into the city
quite unnoticed among the people. Knowing that the time had come for
His "demise in Jerusalem," He chose to announce His arrival by riding
in on a donkey. Let there be no mistake. He was a Man with a price on His
head, and He chose to advertise His arrival and His presence. He was a
Man of destiny, and His destiny was about to engulf Him. Here is raw

courage. The Lamb of God is offering Himself for the sacrifice. He is Lamb among lambs, and ready to be an offering to God for the sin of the world. Later this very day He will drive the moneychangers and the sheep sellers from the temple courts, that the area of choice by the people might be narrowed to only Himself. Before the week is out, the chief priests and the scribes and Pharisees will choose Him, purchase Him for thirty pieces of silver, and engineer His sacrifice.

Just now He crosses the valley from Bethany and approaches the city gates. There are those who recognize Him and spread the word of His arrival. The word speeds like fire in the wind through the city, that Jesus of Nazareth, the same who heals all manner of diseases, is coming. Many go out to meet Him. They are ecstatic. "Keep the donkey's feet off the dirty road," someone cries as he throws his mantle on the road. Others follow suit. Some pull down palm branches to line the street. Amid the commotion the cry goes up, "Blessed be the King that comes in the name of the Lord." They do remember His story of the kingdom of God. They hailed Him as their King. One wonders how many of these same people before the praetorium of Pilate's city quarters would cry out, "We have no king but Caesar."

The cry goes out, "Peace in heaven, and glory to God in the highest." That sounds like the song of the angels on Bethlehem's plains— excepting that the angels had sung about peace on earth among men of good will, while these people speak of peace in heaven.

St. Luke's Gospel offers a reason for the excitement and the praise of the people: "They praised God with a loud voice for all the mighty works that they had seen." Whether this was a true faith-filled people looking for the heavenly King to save His people or whether it was a people looking for a king to offer relief from their earthly domination, the fact remains, Jesus' purpose has been served. There was no question He was in the city. The hour of the Passion was at hand.

The path of the procession ends at the temple. But the path in reality ends at the cross. Jesus walks the real path in kingly mien. Through the trial He conducts Himself with majesty. Let come what may, He is in charge. The temple and Roman guard arrested Him in the garden of prayer. "Whom do you seek?" He asks. "Jesus of Nazareth," they answer. "I am He!" Jesus is very much in control. He is taken to the chief priest's home and before the Sanhedrin. He is accused of blasphemy and condemned to die—by His church. He stands before Pilate and Herod. He is beaten at the whipping post and mocked by ruthless soldiers. He is led to the praetorium, a woeful looking Man. He watches Pilate slip out of responsibility even as he condemns Him to the cross. Always, always, He bears Himself in kingly fashion. Always, in the midst of the raging tempest about Him, He is in charge.

The executioners go about their grisly business; He prays for them. The fellow on the cross next to Him needs comfort; He promises Paradise. His mother stands near the cross; He provides for her. The darkness comes; He enters hell for the justification of the sinful world; He is altogether alone, for even the Father has shut Him out. Yet He is in charge. When the sun breaks through the darkness, He announced the awesome truth. "It is finished!" The sin of the world had been borne away. He had taken the world's sin, even as the plan had required, into His own body on the tree. He had borne the consequences of the Father's judgment against it. Though utterly exhausted in body and in soul, He announced to all who will listen, "It is finished!"

And all the while, He is in control. All the while He acts majestically. All the while, He is indeed King Jesus. All the while He is Christ, the Anointed of God. All the while He is the very Son of God. "Sometimes it causes me to wonder, wonder!" the old spiritual goes. Indeed it does. Who would have thought that God could be like that? Who has a God who has done that—for the world? Sometimes it causes me to wonder.

It is a bit difficult to think of Jesus' impending death as He rides into Jerusalem. We really don't want to hear about death. It's better to have Jesus riding in triumph. It is better to hear the crowd shouting His praise. It's better to shut out the Passion for another day. Who wants to think of His death, when a parade is going by? Yet those who examined the church year have "rechristened" this day the Sunday of the Passion and assigned the reading of the Passion account to it.

Still the urge to make this a day of celebration persists—and we do have something to celebrate. We are living in the days after the cross. We know something of Jesus as the King of kings; we know Him as the Savior of saviors. We know Him as Lord. We are forgiven sinners. We are justified by God and before God. We wear the robes of Christ's righteousness even now. We have beheld the Lamb of God led as a sheep to the slaughter. We know He died for us. It is our joy to celebrate, to stand in remembrance and shout His praises. Hosanna to the Son of David! Blessed be the King who comes in the name of the Father. No, more than that. Blessed be the Son of God who came to redeem us for the Father. Peace in heaven and glory in the highest. Nay, more than that. Glory in heaven, and peace on earth—in the hearts of men and women and between for those who will place Him between themselves.

So cast your palm branches before Him. The Lamb of God is on the way to the slaughtering. Ah, the suffering and death are long past. Cast your palms before Him, raise your hearts and voices in adoration and praise. Behold, the Lamb who is King and the King who is the Lamb of God, is passing by.

In the Upper Room, the Lamb

(Maundy Thursday)

Text: Luke 22:14-15

Dear Christian Friends,

The day for the celebration of the Feast of Easter was set by the church in the days of the Council of Chalcedon in 451 A.D. Since it was desirable to celebrate the great feast on a Sunday, the church developed a formula for establishing the Sunday on which it should be observed. The Jewish Passover is determined by the lunar month calendar and is commemorated among them on a day determined by the phases of the moon. Since Jesus celebrated the Passover with His disciples just before His death, it was decided that the resurrection of Jesus should be celebrated the first Sunday after the full moon on or after March 21, or on the following Sunday if the full moon occurs on a Sunday. Once the Easter date is established, all church year celebrations fall into place from Ash Wednesday to Pentecost. So it is that the Passover ritual and the Easter Feast are always in proximity. Periodically the Passover falls on one or the other of the great Christian days of commemoration—Maundy Thursday, Good Friday. The two celebrations, Easter and the Passover, may touch as two days touch each other; they do not occur on the same day.

It is perhaps strange that we should speak of these things on the holy night when we commemorate the events in the upper room, the night on which our Lord was betrayed. It is precisely in the same way as the touching days that the old covenant touches the new covenant, that the Passover lamb as type touches Christ as the new Passover Lamb reality. It is in the upper room that the old ends and the new is given us. But we are ahead of the story.

The people of the Land of Goshen in the delta country of the Nile were ordered by God to prepare for their journey to freedom. They were to select and kill a lamb without blemish, to smear its blood on the lintels of their doorposts, to roast the lamb, and to stand ready to leave the country. That night the angel of death slew the firstborn in every house in Egypt not stained with the blood of the lamb. In the ensuing tragedy among the Egyptians, the slaves, under the guidance and leadership of Moses, left the land of their bondage . . . for freedom in the wilderness, and eventually the promised land. So momentous was the event in their history that it was celebrated with ritual reenactment for the next centuries (and with refinements to this very day).

In Jesus' day when pilgrims flocked to holy Jerusalem for the Passover, the great city teemed with people. Lambs raised for the

61

commemorative feast were herded into the city, sold to the pilgrims, prepared for the feast. One of them was singled out for the Passover celebration in the Upper Room. Jesus Himself arranged the meal and the place where He could gather with the Twelve. He had an urgent necessity to be with His beloved Twelve and to eat the Passover with them. He must seize the time lest the many things he had on his mind to say and do for them should not be said and done. They must know His love for them, His concern for them once He stepped into His suffering. His worry over their consternation at His death.

More possibly the time had come for that which the evangelists write and which has become our record of the institution of the Lord's Supper. Now the type must give way to the Reality, the lamb of the Passover must at last cease its function as a figure for the Lamb, our Passover, who was sacrificed for us. Jesus washed the disciples' feet. He spoke to them on the necessity for faithfulness. He prayed for them. He moved to the table and sang the Passover hymns with them. He moved into the ancient ritual of questions and answers, of herbs and wine, of eating the Passover lamb.

This is the picture, the drama, the starkness of that hour.

The servant brought the Passover lamb, spitted and roasted, up the stairs to the banquet hall. The eyes of all the disciples followed its course across the room. A servant moved dishes and glasses to make room for it on the table in front of Jesus.

Memories were stirred. They remembered Moses and the terrible stories of the slavery their ancestors endured and their fathers had so often related to them. They thought of the long years since the flight from Egypt and the struggle for the new land. David, and Solomon, Orpah and Ruth came to mind, and the promises of the Messiah, this Jesus who sat before them.

Jesus' eyes, too, followed the lamb as it was carried in. His heart pounds as it is set before Him. Even as this lamb "was led to the slaughter," so must He be led to the cross and death this night. He reaches for His portion of the little lamb and He eats. The taste is bitter in His mouth.

He will go forth shortly from this room to the prayers in the garden, to the betrayal, the heinous trial, to the ignominious death. He will be excommunicated by the church, expunged from the nation, denied by humanity, and forsaken of His Father. He will make atonement for the sin of the world, for our sins, for my sins, this Lamb chosen by God for the redemption of the world.

For a thousand years the paschal lamb had stood as type. Its function ended there in the Upper Room. The Reality had come indeed. The shadow portending the body had ceased its function; the body had arrived.

The Lamb of God took bread and blessed it. "This is My body broken for you," He said. He took wine and gave it to them saying, "This is My blood, given and shed for you." "Do this in remembrance of Me," He said. "This is the *new* covenant in My blood," He announced. Yea, this night the old covenant, marked with conditions, prescribed by laws, dependent on the faithfulness of men, was superseded by a new covenant, made possible by the death of Jesus—for us—dependent altogether upon the grace of God in Christ Jesus.

We are come together this night to remember—lambs and the Lamb, the shedding of His blood and the breaking of His body. We are come together to rejoice in the new covenant with our Lord, announced this night so long ago. We are come together to remember His suffering and death, for the mere act of eating and drinking bread and wine without its institution and its setting carries little purpose.

We are not bound to the past. We are come together because we have a deep need to be with Jesus, who in, with, and under the bread and wine comes to us, enters us, fills us. His very presence in the bread and wine are for our strengthening in the faith, for our forgiveness, for our peace. We are come together because we need each other, for the presence of each of us strengthens all the others of us. We bring the Christ in us to each other. We share the common bond of faith.

Nor are we bound to the present. We are come together because we share a destiny as sons and daughters of God, as brothers and sisters of the Christ. The tables are set in the Kingdom. The feast is now ready. One by one we slip from this vale of tears to find our seats at the end-time Supper of the Lamb. Together we look up and beyond this life to the life that is to come for those who are His people.

The Passover touches Maundy Thursday, the old covenant touches the new, the Paschal lamb touches the Lamb, we sinners touch our Christ. God's desire has been fulfilled. We are saved through Christ. The heavens rejoice.

Come for all things are now ready.

On Calvary, the Lamb

(Good Friday)

Text: 1 Corinthians 5:7

Fellow Believers in Christ,

The celebration of the Passover brought people into the Holy City by the tens of thousands. Josephus, historian, estimates the numbers of pilgrims at 2½ million at the time of Jesus. Because it was the high holy day, all lodging was free. The city was literally "booked solid." Finding a room was virtually impossible.

Sheep farmers brought their animals to the markets of the great city.

The same historian claims that 256,000 sheep had been driven there in preparation for the Passover sales.

Priests were everywhere in evidence, for it was their task to slaughter the sheep. With a deft slip of the knife they slit the jugular vein of the hapless animal, letting its blood flow. They were connoisseurs. They knew sheep. Their practiced eyes surveyed the animal to certify its use at the Passover meal. They were frightfully busy the day before the Passover.

The chief priest was busy, too. He was choosing his "sheep" for the slaughter the day before the Passover. He found the sheep of his choice in the Garden of Gethsemane. That is, his minions did. They brought Him to the priests with thongs binding his wrists. The high priest's biggest problem was how to do the slaughter without staining his priestly garments.

This was accomplished in the end by accusing the Victim before Pontius Pilate. Pilate was unsympathetic to the whole idea and tried to be uncooperative. But pressures of politics prevailed and he finally acquiesced. He washed his hands of the "Pretender to power," this Jesus of Nazareth, in an old Jewish rite (Deut. 21:6; Ps. 26:6) to signify his innocence in the murder that was taking place. The chief priest understood the gesture and accepted its intent. "His blood be on us and our children, not on you, Pilate." They didn't notice the blood stains on their priestly robes.

That is how the Good Shepherd became the "sheep for the slaughter," that day when sheep were slaughtered for the Passover. That is how Jesus, the Christ, came to be on a cross on the hill of execution. That is how He became our Passover. That is how He was sacrificed. That answers the question: where.

And that is perhaps the how, but it is not truly why. That is where but not who. The key to the answer to the "who" question is in those two small words at the end of our text, "for us." Therein lies the awesome story of the heart of God. "God would have all men to be saved." "God so loved the world that He gave His only begotten Son." "God spared not His own Son but delivered Him up for us all."

"For us" sends us back to creation, back to the supreme compliment the Creator paid His noble creation, man and woman. "I will give my man and woman freedom to choose between Me and Satan," said God.

Satan came seducing. His sly words were before the pride of God's creation. Man, O tragic day, failed God's testing. Man ate of the tree of the knowledge of good and evil. Man brought God's righteous judgment, God's wrath, upon himself. The floodgate of sin was opened. Sin asserted itself. Like an evil tide it swept humanity. The Holy Word is quite explicit about its extent. We are all covered only as with "filthy rags." "There is not a just man upon earth that doeth good and sinneth not, no not one." "The wages of sin is death."

64

But God faced a horrible dilemma. His justice is absolute. It is perfect. It cannot be tempered with mercy or abrogated by love . . . and remain perfect justice. God loves His creation. Love must demonstrate total commitment, absolute liability, for its object. God loved His willful creation. How to be at once totally just and love like that . . .

See the Lamb, the sacrificial Lamb on Calvary? He hangs on a cross between two crucified thieves. They mock Him with terrible words, the people milling round, the pilgrims passing on the highway, the thieves crucified with Him. "Hail, king of the Jews! If you are the Son of God . . ." Watch. The sun is going dark . . . a cloud? an eclipse? Ay, it is the dark at noonday the prophets had long ago spoken of. In the darkness the railing has stopped. It is quiet on the hill. In the darkness and quiet, in the terror of the hour, a voice from the cross, "My God, My God, why hast Thou forsaken Me?"

We were speaking of dilemmas and solutions a moment ago. We must speak of expiation. John used the word in an epistle (1 John 2:2). The word he used meant, literally, the meeting place of forgiveness. Something of that must be heard in the understanding of "expiation." "He is the expiation for our sins, and not for ours only but also for the sins of the whole world." Substitute John's word for ours. "Jesus is the meeting place for forgiveness!" Just there is God's solution to the dilemma between what justice demanded and what love was willing to do.

Justice, justification, are focused in God's cross and God's Passover Lamb. Judas, Caiaphas, Herod, Pilate, the multitude, may have played their part in engineering the death of Jesus. It is God who devised the plan. It is the Son who carried out the plan. By the stripes, by the bonds, by the nails and spear—and the darkness and the cry that pierced it— justice is served—by Him—for us.

The surface words come easily, the deep thoughts come only after struggle with the record. What price the forgiveness merited by Christ? Think of an angry God. Think of God's wrath against sin boiling beyond all imagination. Think of abandonment complete and absolute. Think of hell and its most aweful terrors. Think of Satan, dancing in triumph, and of all his minions singing the victory songs of hell . . . around the Christ. My God! Why—how could You thus abandon Him?

It is almost too much to speak of these things. The very angels of heaven are silent. The patriarchs and saints in glory dare not stir. The Father has offered up His Son in the interests of justification, of His perfect justice.

If love is unlimited liability here is the perfect example of it. Such is the liability, the love, of the Father—and of His only begotten Son—for His creation, for us, for me, that He spared not His own Son—that the Son did not grasp His own life but offered Himself for us.

Now you see why St. John speaks of the cross as the meeting place for forgiveness, as the expiation for our sins. Justice and love meet there. They meet in Christ. And there we meet God in His forgiveness. There is no other such meeting place.

Do you seek peace from your sins of the past that return again and again to disturb you? Take them to the cross, to Jesus, and find surcease from their nagging. Do you have besetting sins that shame you? Meet God at the cross to find there help in breaking their hold on you. Are you afraid of temptations that loom in tomorrow's darkness? Find strength in the love and power that comes from the place where you meet God and His Christ.

The message of that first Good Friday is that Jesus died, no, rather Christ, the anointed One, the Son of God, died. But it is far more than that. The message of Good Friday and its cross is that Christ died—for us. Christ our Passover has been sacrificed—for us.

Two and a half million visitors to the city—and the city's population as well—and for most of them it's business as usual . . . keeping shop, preparing for the Passover, milling around a crucifixion, carrying out orders. In the midst of them Christ was crucified. Only a few observed it.

Two hundred and fifty-six thousand sheep, shadows of things to come, but the body that the shadows portend is spitted on a cross and exposed to hell's fires.

Today it's business as usual, in the shops and stores, on the highways and resorts. Many businesses are closed. Good Friday has become a legal holiday. A long weekend. What does the day mean?

Christ our Passover is sacrificed for the human race. Christ our Passover is sacrificed for you.

Easter

Vivit! the Lamb

(Easter Day)

Text: Revelation 5:11-14

Dear Friends in and of the Living Christ,

To come to this day of radiant splendor from the humdrum rhythms of life, or to come to it without the stark, bleak background against which it is laid in Scripture, is to deprive oneself of all that makes it glorious. Vivit! He lives.

It would be well for us to retrace, however briefly, the terrible events that precede it, much the same as a Part II section of a television program does to bring the viewer up to the point where the new section begins. This is precisely what John, the Seer, hears in his vision when he reports the song of the four creatures and the elders (v. 9).

During the Lenten week-night services (or Sundays in Lent) we have been noting a theme that runs through Scripture and which we have identified as "the Lamb motif." Again and again the lamb occurs through the Old Testament at crucial moments in Israel's history. Abel offers a lamb at the first "worship" event recorded in Genesis. Abraham is tested when he was bidden by God to offer Isaac, his only son, only to be relieved of the testing when a ram was found in the brambles. At the Exodus, a lamb was to be killed and eaten, its blood smeared on the doorposts on the evening just before the great movement out of Egypt. The angel of death "passed over" the blood-marked houses and tents. Isaiah sings of the Lamb who was dumb before the shearers and on whom the iniquity of us all was laid. Whether or not the ancient people found the lambs of Abel, of Abraham, of Isaiah prefigures of the Messiah, there can be no doubt of the purpose of these lambs. They were a type of Christ, "a shadow of things to come," as St. Paul calls such things.

John the Baptizer certainly picks up the picture, the type. At the Jordan he cried out, "Behold, the Lamb of God that taketh away the sin of the world!" and the type falls into perspective. On Maundy Thursday the lamb as type confronts Christ as antitype in the Upper Room when the roasted Passover lamb was placed before Him. St. Paul wrote those memorable words to the Corinthian Christians, "Christ our Passover is sacrificed for us" (1 Cor. 5:7). We noted that fact only last Friday, when we spoke of the awesome death of Jesus, the Christ. He was indeed led as a lamb to the slaughter. Like a lamb he was spitted on a cross, and like a lamb set before the flames, He was exposed to the "fires" of hell. What else can the "My God, My God, why hast Thou forsaken Me?" mean but that God had cast Him out of His presence, that God had abandoned Him to hell—for us.

He died on the cross. St. John and the other biographers of Jesus, took great pains to establish that. They portray His last escaping breath as He "yielded up the ghost." They tell us a Roman soldier thrust the spear into His side. We can with them visualize the blood already coagulated, oozing from the spear-thrust wound. They tell us He was washed and bound in the winding sheet. There was no question about His condition. The centurion, standing by, speaks the only eulogy for Christ, "This *was* a righteous man and the Son of God."

The women came early—with the rising of the sun—to finish the task, left undone on Friday, of adding the pungent spices to the lifeless body of Jesus. "Who shall roll us away the stone?" they wondered, but hurried toward the Garden nonetheless. They arrived at last. The Garden is empty. The Roman soldiers left to guard the tomb have gone. And horror of horrors—no, wonder of wonders—they see that the stone has been rolled away from the entrance to the grave. An angel, brilliant and glorious, stands before them. "He is not here. He lives! even as He said!" So the exultant news breaks upon the world. Christ lives! The Lamb sacrificed for us lives!

Some fundamental questions are essential to making Scripture yield its depths. They are to be addressed to any event, any statement, recorded by the Spirit for our learning. In all meditation on the passion and resurrection of our Lord, these are necessary. What does all this mean to/for God the Father? What does this mean to God the Son? The third is vital—what does this mean to me? Here is an angel messenger with the proclamation "Jesus is risen even as He said." Let's answer the questions.

The Resurrection is God's doing and it is marvelous in our eyes. God, who sent Jesus into the world, who gave Him up to die, who abandoned Him to hell that our sins and the sin of the world might be expiated, God—raised Him from the dead. God would not let His holy One see corruption. Jesus, the Christ, had been faithful to the trust, faithful to the plan, faithful even unto death, the death of the cross. God reached into the tomb and touched His lifeless body. God gave Him life. God gave Him glory.

There is no question about it, God accepted the suffering and death of His only begotten Son. God heard the cry from the cross, addressed to Him alone, yet heard clearly by all at the cross: "It is finished!" The plan conceived in the councils of the Trinity before the foundations of the world were laid had been brought to completion. Justice had been served. Love had triumphed. God accepted the atoning work of Christ. He will not allow His Son to see corruption. God is faithful to His promises. God is trustworthy. Because of the resurrection of Jesus we can have confidence in God.

Vivit! Christ our Passover is sacrificed for us. Vivit! Christ our Passover lives. God raised Him from the dead, and we too shall live.

And what of Jesus, the Christ. We could, of course, speak of His appearances—to Mary, to the Emmaus disciples, to the Twelve. They are part and parcel of the Resurrection stories. We could speak of His ascension into glory, but there is a day reserved for that 40 days hence. Rather, however, let us speak of the Lamb as St. John sees Him in the vision called Revelation. The text I have chosen this morning is that exciting portion of the vision when the Lamb opens the book of the seven seals. No one in all of glory has been able to open it. The Lamb steps forward and takes the book. The 4 living creatures and the 24 elders compose and sing a new song.

> Worthy art Thou to take the scroll and to open its seals, for Thou wast slain and by Thy blood didst ransom men for God from every tribe and tongue and people and nation, and hast made them a kingdom and priests to our God, and they shall reign on earth. (Rev. 5:9-10 RSV)

The whole company of heaven—the angels hovering about the throne, the myriads of angels, the whole company of the patriarchs, sing the chorus—in praise of the Lamb. The sound of it must have been exceedingly beautiful, the power of it enough to shake the walls of glory, the glory of it beyond all imagination.

> Worthy is the Lamb who was slain, to receive power and wealth and wisdom and might and honor and glory and blessing! (V. 12)

And still the song is not finished. The chorus is picked up by everything on earth, under the earth, and in the sea. The glorious sound filled all creation as it praised and honored the Lamb.

> Blessing and honor and glory and power be given to Him who sits upon the throne, and to the Lamb, for timeless ages! (V. 13)

When at last the great chorus came to an end, an "Amen" was added, quietly, I should think, melodic certainly, by the four living creatures. And the elders fell down and worshiped the Lamb.

The Lamb of God, sacrificed on Calvary for the sin of the world, had accomplished the plan of God for man's redemption. He paid for the sins of mankind at God's price. "Wherefore God has highly exalted Him!" Wherefore the saints and angels in glory sing His everlasting praises.

Wherefore He is appointed King of kings and Lord of lords.

Worthy is the Lamb to be Lord of history. That is what the little book that was sealed with the seven seals and which none could open save the Lamb is all about. The remainder of Revelation is about the Lamb's lordship of history. He would, indeed, "bring everything together in Christ" (Eph. 1:10). History would from henceforth and forever be under His dominion.

Worthy is the Lamb to be the Lord of the church. Every person who is in and of the church, by the power of the Holy Spirit, would call Jesus Lord (1 Cor. 12:3). He is ruler of everything, the Head of the church (Eph. 1:22-23). He is our Lord by right of redemption born of obedience to the Father and out of love for us sinners.

Worthy is the Lamb to be Lord of the nations, acknowledged so or not. He is the head of every sovereignty and power (Col. 2:10). "Beautiful Savior! Lord of the nations!" we sing in the beloved hymn of the Bohemian peasants.

Worthy is the Lamb to be Lord over the unseen powers. He preached to the spirits in prison (1 Peter 3:19); God has made the angels and dominions and powers His subjects (Eph. 1:21).

Worthy is the Lamb to be Lord over death. At Calvary He conquered death and all its terrors. Vivit! He lives! He has abolished death (2 Tim. 1:10). He has conquered the last of the enemies and destroyed death (1 Cor. 15:26). He has given us the victory over death (1 Cor. 15:55-57). We too shall live!

Worthy is the Lamb to be the Lord of glory. He sits at the right hand of the Father. The hallelujah choruses of the angels are sung to Him and in His honor. He will come again in all His glory with all His holy angels (Matt. 25:31).

Worthy is the Lamb to be the Lord of Judgment, for in love He became our substitute under the Law and the judgment of God. He is given the right of judgment over the world, over our souls (Matt. 25:31), when He takes the seat of His throne of glory, and all who are covered with His righteousness can dare to stand in the Judgment unafraid.

"Worthy is the Lamb to receive blessing and honor and glory and power"—must, indeed, be part and parcel of our song, for He who is Lord is our Lord, who has redeemed us.

And what of us, we who are the redeemed? We are made a kingdom of priests for our God. We reign as kings upon the earth. That promise is not new. It was part of the old covenant at Mount Sinai when God came for His people Israel. "You shall be to me a kingdom of priests" (Ex. 19:5-6). In the new covenant St. Peter could write of the followers of Jesus, "You are a chosen race, a royal priesthood, a holy nation, God's own people" (1 Peter 2:9 RSV). John hears the mighty truth again in our Revelation text: You, My people, are a kingdom of priests. Priests with the privilege of prayer! Priests who present your bodies a living sacrifice to God! Priests who have the privilege of the Throne Room. Priests who are at the disposal of the King of kings. And you are kings upon the earth—in Christ. Rulers of your destiny—in Christ. Subject to no one—save Christ.

Vivit, He lives! Christ our Passover is sacrificed for us. Vivit, He lives! The whole Christian church on earth, the whole community of saints, the whole kingdom of God, is predicated on the Easter fact. By the grace of God and the power of the Holy Spirit, we have predicated our lives and our futures, our eternity, on that fact. And one day, or should I say, one eternity, by the sheer grace of God and by the death and resurrection of Jesus, the Anointed of God, we will hear the angel chorus. We will know the tune when we arrive in glory. We will join in the singing. "Blessing and honor and glory and power be unto Him who sits upon the throne, and unto the Lamb, forever."

Do You Love Me? Feed My Lambs

(A Sunday of Easter)

Text: John 21:15-17

Dear Friends in Christ,

When one reads the lessons and the Gospels for the three-year series, one is impressed with two primary conclusions about them. They are charged with reasons for repentance and faith in Jesus Christ, and they are guidelines for living the life expected of God's people. In some of them the mighty deeds of God, especially in Christ, are front and center—a miracle perhaps, or a parable, or an event in the life of Christ. In others there are goals to strive for in living within the freedom wherewith Christ has made us free.

But then, that is exactly what is to be expected. Matthew wrote to his Hebrew peers with a view to encourage them to accept the Messiah, the Christ, who had come in the person of Jesus. Luke writes to encourage Theophilus to and in the faith which is in Jesus as Savior. Paul certainly, though he writes his letters to Christian congregations, consistently urges them in and to the faith and life becoming God's people. Beyond and above such human considerations is the Holy Spirit, who inspired those holy men to write that He might have a tool through which He could call a people together for God.

This familiar text can therefore be expected (as all texts do) to be a call to discipleship and an exhortation to deep commitment. "What are you saying to me, text?" Each of us hears the text speak to him according to his familiarity with it and in accord with his personal life condition. As

71

preacher I can expound the text from my study and meditations on it; I can suggest a few applications of it from my personal experiences. You, as hearer of the Word, must absorb what your personal familiarity and personal experience allow.

The time of the incident in our text is after the glorious resurrection of our Lord Jesus. The disciples had gone back to the sea, back to their boats, back to their nets. In their three years with Jesus they seemed to have lost their knack for fishing, for they labored all night and caught nothing. Jesus appeared on the shore, commanded them to cast their nets into the sea—at a most ridiculous place and time of day. Wonder of wonders, they caught a great draft.

Jesus breakfasted with them on the beach, roasting the fish and toasting their bread over a little fire. The conversation around the fire was, I should think, rather noncommittal, since none is recorded. None, that is, except the little one-on-one conversation between Peter and Jesus.

The conversation begins with a question, "Simon, son of John, do you love Me more than these?"

Peter hesitated for a moment. His mind, always quick as lightning, raced . . . like, they say, one's mind will do in a dire circumstance. "What a freighted question that one is!" he thought. "He's been talking about love ever since I have known Him. He reads too much into that word for me!" "Love" needs a definition. One of the simplest is to give someone or something first place in one's life. This woman is more important to me than all the women of the world. I love this car. I love this dog. Love singles out; it narrows down from all possible cars, or dogs, or people, and centers on this one.

More specifically, and perhaps more eruditely, love, whatever else it may harbor as a word, is taking ultimate liability for, giving total commitment to. "Whoever loves father or mother, son or daughter, more than Me is not worthy of Me," Jesus had said. "Sell all that you have," He told a young lawyer. "That means," Peter could have reasoned, "leave behind my faithful wife, forfeit my boats and nets, forget my little house by the sea. It means to forsake all others and all else for Him."

Simon's hesitation hardly showed, but it was there. In a moment or two he took his stance. "Yes, Lord, you know I am Your friend." Now I know that King James and the Revised Standard Version and other translations render Peter's answer differently. They have Peter saying, "You know I love You"—but the original uses one word for "love" when Jesus speaks, and another when Peter answers. There is, unquestionably, a play on words between the question and the answer, but more, there is a larger difference between the requirement of Jesus and the willingness of Peter to rise to the requirement. (Some recent translations use the word "friend" in Peter's reply.)

Being a friend and having a friend is indeed a wondrous gift. A friend is someone you can walk hand in hand with, someone you enjoy being with, someone with whom you can share confidences. Peter, no doubt, is remembering the long walks and good talks they had had together as they toured the land. He is remembering the retreats they had had together and how much he had enjoyed and appreciated that. He is thinking of the confidence Jesus had shown Him by taking him up on the Mount of Transfiguration and into the Garden of Gethsemane. But Peter couldn't bring himself to the idea of total commitment. That was asking too much.

"Feed my lambs," Jesus said. Then He repeated the question, using the same word a second time, "Do you love Me?"

Simon Peter's mind races again. He remembers the night in the Upper Room when Jesus had told them all, "Greater love has no man than that a man lay down his life for his friends—ye are My friends." Does love require that of me? And there was that terrible crucifixion time where He prayed for those ruthless men charged with His execution, "Father, forgive them." "No," Peter thought, "for that I am not ready." His answer was the same, and even as he said it, there was a shade of anger in his reply. He hadn't changed position. "You know I am Your friend."

Friends are precious to life. Most people have very few of them in a lifetime. In fact, who has one or two bosom friends in a lifetime is fortunate. Peter surely considered Jesus such a Friend. "Even if everyone forsakes You, Jesus, I will not." "I'll defend you against Malchus with the sword if necessary. You are my Friend. Isn't that enough?"

Jesus said, "Then feed My sheep."

But now comes the third time of asking—and Jesus changes words to use the one of Peter's choice. "Are you My friend, Simon, son of John?"

The question implied so much. Peter hadn't understood the lesson of the Mount of Transfiguration. Peter couldn't grasp the necessity for His death on the cross. Peter fell asleep in the Garden of Gethsemane. Peter cut off the high priest's servant's ear. Peter denied Him. "Are you My friend?"

"Lord, You know everything. You know I am Your friend." Peter blushed as he said it. The edge on his words was sharper than it had been before. Peter knew he ought to have gone all the way, but somehow he wasn't ready. The little scene and the simple conversation would follow him, haunt him—until a week or two hence when the Holy Spirit would apprehend him; and then, without equivocation, he would commit himself body and soul, life and limb, to Jesus. Only then, at last, was the total commitment that Jesus claimed from Peter there on the shores of Galilee.

Now—Peter is every man. The question of Jesus is His for everyone. "Do you love me more than these?" Have you, without reservation, committed yourself to Jesus? Each of us, I should imagine, will do what Peter did, hesitate the way he did, say what he said. Loving like Jesus did can make unbelievably difficult demands on the lover.

Tradition says that Peter went to Rome on his missionary journey—and was ultimately crucified head down (because he was not worthy to be crucified as was his Lord) because he dared to love Jesus. Peter is only one of many thousands. Bartholomew was flayed, James stoned, Thomas shot through with arrows and a spear . . . for loving Jesus. Times have not changed since then. Thousands have met the martyr's death in our generation! The Russian Revolution had no room for the church or for Christians in its communistic philosophies. China closed its doors to missionaries for many years to rid itself of Christian influences. The South American powers cannot grasp the rebirth and renewal of Roman Catholicism and has tortured priests and martyred other Christians. But the lists are gruesome and the stories tragic. In the midst of them comes the question of Jesus, "Lovest thou Me?" And in the face of them must come our answer to the question. What shall it be?

We are bombarded on all sides with temptations to live outside the morals of our Christian ethic. The world has chosen life-styles contrary to the spirit of Christ. Advertising appeals to our basic Old Adam; the many media that entertain us chose to do so with the sinful and offerings of sinful people. The question will not leave the child of the Most High alone. "Simon—Mary, John, George, Harriet—do you love me?" And most of us, perhaps all of us, protest in Peter's voice, "Lord, You know I am Your friend!"

It is bad enough to to weave one's way through the world of temptations. It must be awesome to face martyrdom for the Gospel's sake. I know I promised faithfulness to death at my confirmation; yet I wonder, were I faced with a cross or stoning or starvation or banishment would I be committed enough, in love enough, to face it? I pray the Holy Spirit that I am; but I pray more, as I am sure you do, that I never ever be put to the testing time.

In the meantime, hopeful of God's affirmative answer to my/our prayers, the lambs must be fed, the sheep led to still waters. There is much to do in the Kingdom, enough and more to supplant the worries about tomorrow or to borrow the future's problems. God who loves us in our Lord Jesus Christ is faithful to us. We must, and by His grace and strengthening, we will, seek to be faithful to Him. We will, I pray, seek to say from a deep commitment, "Jesus, Lord, You know all things. You know I love You."

The Lamb/the Shepherd

(A Sunday of Easter)

Text: John 10:11

Dear Christian Friends,

It may seem strange to begin a sermon with an English lesson, but there is sufficient reason to do so. There is a manner of speaking, a tool of rhetoric it is called, in which a person, an event, a thing, is described by using one idea to help understand another. One such tool is the image—as when we say, "My dad is a fossil, a brick, a square." Each image conveys an aspect of "my dad." Metaphors, another tool, are implied comparisons in which a figurative term is used for, or identified with, the literal term, as when one says, "My dad is a lion in the business world." And there are similies, which compare two unlike things. An example might be, "My dad is like Gibraltar." Each figure of speech says something about "my dad," and helps the hearer to see him this way or that.

I mention this tool of rhetoric because we have been using it freely for the last few weeks. In the evening (Sunday morning) services of Lent we used the device with Scriptural permission and spoke of Jesus as a lamb led to the slaughter. "As a sheep before her shearers—so He." "Behold the Lamb of God," John cried as Jesus appeared on the bank of the Jordan River. It was a fine way to speak of Jesus in His passion, for the idea of Jesus as Lamb conveys many aspects of Jesus as He suffers and dies. There is something of the choice of the lamb without blemish and without spot for the Passover and the sacrifice, in the Father choosing His Son to bear the burden of judgment against the world's sin. The lamb's docility fits Jesus as He voluntarily assumes our sin-burden, and vicariously becomes the "sacrifice" we should have been. He was defenseless before His accusers; He prayed for His executioners even as they lifted their sledges to drive home the rusty spikes, "Father, forgive them." The simile, the metaphor is strong and it was helpful.

But the image and the simile can change and still carry truth. That is the nature of the tool. Jesus can be likened, as He Himself does, to a shepherd, just as Isaiah and the Baptist see Him as a lamb. The shepherd loves his sheep; he identifies with them; he is solicitous of them; he defends them; he is ready to give his life for them. The step from such marks of a shepherd to Jesus as Good Shepherd is short and easily taken. David did it so naturally in the 23rd Psalm, "The Lord is my Shepherd, I shall not want." There in simple yet brilliant poetry he wrote of the beautiful things a shepherd does for his sheep, and we hear him speaking of God, or of the Christ, who leads, nourishes, protects us.

75

So now the image changes back again to the Good Shepherd picture. (We will reserve the right to use the "lamb" metaphor later on, since the Scripture does precisely that, especially in Revelation, where the Lamb is front and center.) As the picture, the image, changes, we become sheep of the flock again, with all the problems of sheep. This fact remains constant for the sheep—they have a Good Shepherd, not a hireling.

We may not like the picture. "Me a sheep, indeed!" Sheep are such defenseless creatures. No bark, no bite, no claws, no aggressiveness. Just sheep. They have no strength. They don't pull wagons; they nibble on the grasses; all they seem to do is eat, sleep, and grow wool. They follow blindly. If it weren't so demeaning, one might even say they are stupid animals. A little reflection, however, makes that picture apt, especially if the enemy is seduction, the ruthless devil, or the certainty of death. What defenses have we against such enemies. Or remember the Russian Revolution, when so many people were forced to take the rule of so few, and have not been able to lift a finger against them since. And how about the dictates of fashion, the place to go, the in thing to do, the hep talk of the moment. The picture is not so poorly drawn at that. We are indeed in need of a Good Shepherd, who with good shepherd concern, watches over us day and night—for a whole lifetime.

Let me say a few words about the metaphor of the shepherd in Scripture—to round out the picture. The sheep are gathered into a flock and the flock is always God's. Jesus is the Good Shepherd, who in turn appoints others to care for His sheep, but the flock always belongs to God. The well-being of the sheep is altogether dependent on the character of the shepherd. He is to bring all the sheep into a single fold, to feed the shepherdless and to gather the lost. In the Old Testament, Israel is the flock; in the New the emphasis is on Jesus and His followers. The core material of the metaphor is the commitment of the Shepherd to His flock, to the point of giving His life for His sheep. The flock, in turn, stands ready to give itself for the Shepherd (Rom. 8:36).

The marks of the good shepherd are clearly drawn in Scripture. He is in mutual confidence with his sheep. He has an individual concern for them; he offers them protection; he feeds them and supplies water for them. He is ready to sacrifice himself on their behalf. Just so Jesus, the Good Shepherd, cares for His Father's flock; thus He cares for us.

By nature we are as lost sheep. The Old Adam in us is responsible for that. Sin has separated us from God and alienated us from the Kingdom. "The Son of Man came seeking the lost." So absolutely dangerous was the search for our souls it cost Him His life. An illustration would put the whole story of His concern into focus.

In Balquhidder one year there was a terrible snowstorm that piled snow in high drifts on the Scottish hillsides. The shepherds went out after the lambs. One shepherd never came home. They looked for him for several days, but he was nowhere to be found. Blinded by the snow, he had fallen, broken and stunned, into the deep snow. The snow enfolded him in its gentle arms, and his soul was taken home by the Good Shepherd, who so long before had also laid down His life for the sheep.

The place where it all happened is marked by the villagers. They never pass it without thoughts of that other Good Shepherd whose wandering, foolish sheep we all are. He laid down His life outside the city wall. We are like the good people of Balquhidder when we gather in church to worship and raise our eyes to the hill of our Lord's sacrifice for us. As often as we do, the spirit of sacrifice becomes stronger and the spirit of selfishness is shamed. Life with all its problems and fears becomes a little more tolerable—for the Good Shepherd knows us, knows our fears, our hurts, our lostness. He comforts and protects us as the Scottish sheepherder did for his little lambs.

Are we sinners? The Good Shepherd laid down His life for the sheep, that they might take theirs up again, freed from the heat and burden of their folly before God. Even as He was being crucified the Good Shepherd reached for those who wielded hammer and ropes. Even on the cross He reached across to caress the thief dying on His right. In the fearful darkness, forsaken of the Father, He warded off from us the Father's judgment and the horrible machinations of Satan. And at the end He cried His victory cry for the Father and all of us to hear, "It is finished!" "I have saved My beloved sheep!"

Are we burdened? The Good Shepherd knows our weakness and the cumbering load of care. Vast numbers of sick and hurting sheep have found courage to go on day by day, knowing they were in His care. Vast numbers of sheep with reverses in their affairs of life, have found Him near and deeply concerned with them.

Are we fearful of life's ending? The thought troubled David as he composed the psalm that has comforted endless numbers of the hurting and the dying. "Yea," he wrote, "though I walk *through* [not into] the valley of the shadow of death, I will fear no evil, for Thou art with me; Thy rod and Thy staff, they comfort me." The recent studies of those who have been clinically dead are fascinating. Time and time again those who have come back from their "deadness" have reported gleaming lights and great hope on the other side. Lazarus came back. It is said that he didn't talk much afterwards (no word of his is reported in the Lazarus account). What is there to say when one has had a glimpse of heaven. Paul was caught up into the seventh heaven, but he declines to talk about his experience beyond saying that human language is to sparse to tell what he had seen. "Yes, though I walk through the valley of the shadow of death, Thou art with me."

Images and metaphors have their place as a tool of language and communication. They are meant to convey pictures to help us understand. Yet they cannot be driven past their point of comparison. They make their point, they convey their thought, then they must be abandoned. We are not only as sheep, for instance, we are sons and daughters of the King. We are God's royal priesthood. We are His children, and His brothers and sisters. We are lights on a candlestick and a city on a hill. Each of the images conveys a different facet of our personhood, or suggests a different aspect of our spirituality and life in Christ.

By the same token, the Good Shepherd image of Jesus, the Christ, is only one aspect of Jesus. He, as we suggested earlier in this meditation, is the Lamb of God. And He is so much more in the imagery of Scripture. He is King; He is Vine; He is Light; He is Bridegroom—to mention a few of the many images ascribed to Him. It depends where we are in our thinking and our needs which of the images will help us to understand His relationship to us just then. But of the pictures none is so warm, so comforting, so reassuring to most of us as that warm and wonderful one that David chose and St. Peter cherished—the image of the Good Shepherd. The Lord is my shepherd—what more could the weary, the lonely, the lost, ask for of their Lord, or know of their Lord, than that?

The Ascension of Our Lord

The Wedding Feast of the Lamb

Text: Revelation 19:9 (1-10)

Dear Fellow Servants of the Lord's Christ,

Forty days after His resurrection the days were accomplished that He should return to the Father. He chose a hilltop place near Bethany for the occasion. He reassured His disciples of His continuing presence. He gave them the mandate to preach the Gospel and baptize the nations. He blessed them. Then He was carried up to heaven, disappearing before them. So unexpected, so unusual, so phenomenal was the event they were left speechless and immobile until angels spoke to them and sent them back to Jerusalem.

Who wouldn't stand there looking up at the place where they had seen anyone, let alone Jesus, disappear in the sky? It would be difficult enough to grasp the "mechanics" of such a phenomenon. With all the excitement and hope of the last weeks, holding one enormous event after the others—the Passion and death, the Resurrection, the appearances, the bewilderment about the future—how could one comprehend all that? It would take angels to break the spell!

It strikes me how wonderful it would have been if a gaping hole had been left in the heavens so that we could see past the veil that separates us from the excitement in glory at Jesus' return. It must have been a splendor beyond dreams. The trumpeter angels sounding the arrival, the angel choristers singing, the movement of the Father down the streets of glory to greet His victorious Son—such sights and sounds mankind has never heard, however great the celebrations he might devise.

But hold a moment. There is such a hole—in St. John's Revelation. His apocalyptic vision fires the imagination and fills the believer's heart with anticipation. He sees in his vision the great throne whereon the Father sits in majestic splendor, the cherubim and seraphim hovering round about it. The singing of the angels reaches his ears. "Holy, holy, holy, is the Lord God Almighty, who was and is and is to come!" (Rev. 4:8 RSV). He sees the Lamb (that seemed to have been slaughtered) open the book of the seven seals, the history of the future. He hears again the chorus, singing a descant against the Holy, holy, holy melody. "Worthy is the Lamb to receive power and riches and wisdom and strength and honor and glory and blessing" (Rev. 5:12 KJV).

The visions of John sweep through the terrors wrought by the Lamb as He orders the angels with the bowls and trumpets to destroy the evil powers on the earth. He has glimpses of the faithful martyrs arriving in glory. Then, when at last the earth is conquered, the Lord God Almighty assumes His kingdom, and the angels, in thunderous voices, announce the wedding feast of the Lamb.

The moment, the event, is an absolute climax in the vision. Out of the devastation come the faithful, the church, which is sometimes called the bride of Christ. The church as bride may be one of the lesser metaphors for the church in the New Testament, yet it is used frequently enough in the Bible. Like a bride the church is faithful; she loves, she is obedient, she is loyal. She is adorned in the righteous robes of Christ and with the righteousness of good works which flow from faithfulness to Christ through the power of the indwelling Spirit. The church is the work of the Holy Spirit. She is presented to Christ by the Holy Spirit as the perfect bride, holy and acceptable to Him.

The moment of the vision (glimpsed through the opening that Revelation grants us) is that of the glorious entry into the wedding feast. Imagination is allowed to stretch, for this is apocalyptic material. The Lamb approaches the bride. He smiles at her. He moves to her side. Together they approach the great doors of the banquet hall. The doors swing open. The setting in the hall is nothing short of spectacular. The hall itself, like the walls of the Holy City, are sparkling with precious stones. The table is set with gleaming gold and shining crystal. The floral arrangements of celestial flowers are dazzlingly beautiful. Together the Lamb and His bride enter. They are seated at the wedding table. Even from here the love between them is obvious, their longing for each other is evident. Add the presence of the Lord, our God, the Almighty, to the scene . . . and the angels singing in splendid chorus . . . the swirling arpeggios on the stringed instruments, the music of the spheres. The moment is one of surpassing splendor.

But these are only words that flow from the finite imagination. Surely they are humble guesses of what our Lord has in store for the faithful when the ascended Christ claims His bride for all eternity. Yet it is imagination born from a hint of what is to come as the promises of God work out in the future. These glimpses have sustained the noble martyrs as they forfeited life in time, for the faith, for their Christ. Stephen, noble martyr, saw visions like this even as he was stoned. Surely the army of others martyred for their faithfulness shared such visions of the promises fulfilled. Peter, hanging upside down on his cross, or Hus tied to a pole and burned to death, the 20th-century martyrs put to sword by 20th-century enemies of the cross—they saw the vision. All have, surely, in the hour and the time of their death looked past the Mount of Ascension to see the Lamb who was slaughtered, and hurried through the great doors that seem so ominous to earthbound people, to be forever with the Lord.

The Holy Spirit, who moved the great evangelists to write the story of the Christ, was most consistently concerned that all should come to the knowledge of the saving work and love of the Father and the Son. There is no passage in the four gospels, in the letters of St. Paul, in the lesser epistles without supernatural power. Every miracle, every parable, every saying, every thesis, even those seemingly inane genealogies, pack into themselves the power of the Spirit to convict and convince—if, of course, they are allowed to speak and if they are heard as truth.

The Book of Revelation does no less. It is like the icing on the cake. Even as it unfolds its terrifying judgments, it calls people to repentance. And when it speaks the Gospel it speaks with formidable eloquence. What could better sustain a prophet banished from his country, a man in the terrors of the deep, a woman on a pyre, a lonely prisoner, a missionary in a foreign and hostile land than glimpses of the glory which shall be revealed to us such as the Holy Spirit has provided us in this book of divine power, inspired by the Holy Spirit, and fused with His power.

Now, lest any should miss the point in recording the promise in the bride ready to attend the wedding feast, the Spirit inspires John to write the words of challenge to faithfulness from God the Almighty, Himself. "Write this: Blessed are those who are invited to the marriage supper of the Lamb" (Rev. 19:9 RSV). Then, to clinch the invitation as genuine, "These are true words of God." All the Scriptures, every sermon, all Sunday school lessons, are invitations to all who read or hear them. The invitation goes out to all. "God would have all men to be saved and to come to the knowledge of the truth" (1 Tim. 2:4). The suffering and death of Christ was for the world—for all people. It is the Holy Spirit's task to invite them.

Happy, blessed, the person who clutches the invitation, who carries it through the doors at the end of time. It is his assurance of a place at the wedding banquet.

There is no room for excuses. Jesus told a story about people invited to a feast, undoubtedly in anticipation of the wedding feast of the Lamb. Those invited all began to make excuses. You remember the story. "I have bought a piece of ground, I have only just been married, I have bought me a yoke of oxen." All the excuses are readily translated into the 20th-century idiom—and practice. "I had too much religion as a child. Religion gets in the way of my life-style. We're too tired, too bored, too busy, to become involved." But the list is long, the excuses many. Yes, it is hard. It may cost you your life. The promises, the dividends are incalculable. The risk is worth selling everything to keep your date with eternal destiny. "Blessed are those who are invited." Yes, and far more blessed are they who accept the invitation to the wedding feast.

He was taken up into heaven before them. "Go back to Jerusalem and wait," the angel advised them. Back they went to Jerusalem and devoted themselves to prayer, to the business of replacing Judas, and though Scripture doesn't say it, to the business of their daily bread. It is ever thus. We have our mountaintop experiences. We have time with Jesus. We catch a vision of the splendor of God in His glorious grace and His infinite love. Then it's back to our Jerusalem, back to our daily round. But we are better fit for the routine tasks, better equipped for the uncertainties, and far more ready for the future and what it may bring us. We've had a glimpse through an aperture into glory; we've seen the splendor of the promised wedding feast. We, in faith, have our invitation and we wait for the word that all things are ready. He who was lifted up on a cross has drawn us to Him; He who was lifted up out of sight draws us still, for the Word of God is true and faithful.

Pentecost

I Send You as Sheep

Text: Matthew 10:16

Dear Christian Friends,

The end is the beginning. Just now the festival half of the church year is ending—and the Christian life cycle, is beginning. But it was ever thus. Eden came to an end. Leaving the Garden, Adam and Eve faced the future which demanded a new trust and carried a new hope. The slavery in Egypt came to an end on the night of the Exodus, but a new time of testing in the wilderness loomed ahead. Christ died. Easter came. Even death, which seems so final, is really a beginning—for the Christian in glory, for the unbeliever in hell.

More specifically, the first Pentecost marked the end of Judaism and the beginning of the Christian era for many people. For the disciples it meant the end of their training, and the beginning of their service in the kingdom of God. We celebrate Pentecost because it is the birthday of the church, the beginning of the acts of the Holy Spirit to prepare the bride of Christ for the Bridegroom. From this day the first disciples and all disciples since will do their *sacramentum* (the Latin word for it), that is, take their vows of loyalty and allegiance to the kingdom of God.

St. Luke describes the day in the Pentecost lesson of Acts 2. There was a wind-sound in the city, the same "wind" no doubt that blew across the face of the deep at creation. And the same that came as a "still small wind" at the mouth of Elijah's cave. And the same as that with which Jesus breathed on His disciples when He commissioned them to their task. The Spirit was in the wind-sound, and people moved to its source and found the disciples assembled. There were flames that appeared over the disciples . . . of the same stuff and substance as the pillar of fire that had shielded and led the fleeing Israelites from the Egyptians. And the same that disclosed the presence of God to His people. And the Spirit was in the flame, for the flame was of the Spirit.

Peter stood up to preach the first of the myriad sermons that were to be spoken in the Christian church. He spoke no doubt in his own tongue, but another miracle happened. At least 15 different speaking groups of people were in the Holy City to celebrate the Feast of Weeks . . . and they all heard Peter (and the disciples) speak in their own language. Peter preached of the old prophecies with which his peers had lived for generations. He spoke of Jesus and His message and miracles. Then wonder of wonders, he brought the whole meaning of the Crucifixion into focus. He proclaimed the Resurrection. He called for faith in Jesus, whom God had declared by the Resurrection to be both Lord and God. After his message that day, about 3,000 souls were baptized. What a birthday party!

So, in a thrilling "church service," replete with sermon, the holy Christian church was set in motion, 3,000 strong. So the great plan of the Holy Spirit for evangelizing the world began. Beginning in Jerusalem, the movement gets under way outward to Judea, to Samaria, and to the uttermost parts of the world. Filled with the Holy Spirit, and with the presence of Jesus ("Lo, I am with you alway, even unto the end of the world") and the power of the Spirit, the disciples—and disciples of the disciples—moved into mission. The task was formidable; the work was dangerous. Many times the disciples were to remember their instructions when they were sent on a practice mission by Jesus.

"Behold, I send you out as sheep in the midst of wolves; so be wise as serpents and innocent as doves" (Matt. 10:16). Armed with love and patience, carrying the Gospel of peace, they journeyed into the world. Defenseless sheep they seemed to be. "Wolves" there were aplenty. They moved in faith, by faith, with the faith to conquer the world for Jesus, a dozen men against the multitudes of the nations.

History mixed with legends presents an odyssey stranger than fiction. The moral might easily be drawn that wolves are more powerful than sheep, that evil triumphs. James proclaimed the Gospel of his Lord's death and resurrection in Jerusalem. The "wolves" cornered him at a temple wall and threw him over to the rocks below. He did not die and they stoned him to death. Peter carried the Gospel of Jesus to Rome. The wolf pack closed in and crucified him head down. John, the beloved disciple, was banished to Patmos, by the Roman wolves. He died in Ephesus still the sheep, still proclaiming that love, God's and man's, is the only way to live. Bartholomew was flayed. Thomas was used for target practice and done to death by arrows and spears. The list goes on for the disciples. But it by no means stops there.

Many of the disciples' disciples went out as sheep and met the wolves of the world as they carried on the mission. Paul ran headlong into the wolves at every turn. He was beaten, banished, imprisoned, and finally, he was beheaded. Christian sheep met the persecutions. Rome insisted all people sacrifice to the Roman gods—to receive an identification card to carry. Christians refused to so deny their heavenly Father and their Lord Jesus Christ. They became victims in the Roman games. Nero burned the slums of Rome; the Christians became scapegoats and were summarily put to death.

Through the centuries the terror and the tragedy continued. When some poet authored the familiar and beloved "Te Deum," he took special note of the "noble army of martyrs" who praise the blessed Trinity. In the medieval ages the wolves often wore sheep's clothing, as the churchmen of the time made seeming heretics into unquestioned martyrs of the faith. Nor has the power of the wolfpack or the day of sheep slaughter ended. Our time has its own long list of martyrdoms. Five missionaries seek to make contact with the members of a tribe of South American natives. They land their little plane on a river bank and are killed. (Wondrous story, the missionaries' wives continued their husbands' work and have been successful.) Russian communists closed the churches, and untold numbers of Christians suffered and died in the process. The South American resurgence of faith, since Vatican II allowed the Scriptures in the native tongue, has produced innumerable martyrs. A band of guerillas enter a youth camp retreat and summarily shoot the young men and women.

Tom Dooley, Navy doctor, tells of atrocities against Christians by the Vietcong. A priest is found by the acolytes arriving for service, hanging by his ankles and severely beaten. The priest was subsequently nursed back to health—only to return to his people. A group of schoolchildren have their eardrums pierced, and their teacher has his tongue cut out for praying the Lord's prayer.

If all the truth were known of the slaughter of Christ's sheep, the monumental facts would stagger us. It is the wonder of the faith that it still moves men and women to mission, to face the unknown, to face death, in order that the proclamation of the suffering and death, the resurrection and ascension of Jesus for the sin of the wolfpack might be known. It is the power of the Spirit to impel the faithful to such lengths for the Gospel of peace. Peter's sermon that called 3,000 to repentance and faith and Baptism is still the core stuff of the message. Peter's martyrdom is still symbol of so many Christians' martyrdom in this our generation.

These things are said to you this morning because it is the birthday of the church, the beginning of the Christian mission to the world. They are said that you may recall your baptismal vow, reaffirmed at your confirmation: Will you continue steadfast in the faith which is in Jesus Christ, and suffer all, even death, rather than to fall away from it? Our faith in Jesus Christ, Lord of all and our Lord, our Life, is always in the balance pan. We are spared the ravaging wolves of ruthless rulers and ruthless men, most of us anyway. We probably, most of us anyway, will not face martyrdom. Thank God.

Yet in our simpler, quieter lives, there are still the wolves in sheep's clothing. The temptations of life are very much with us. We are easily taken in. Listen to news reports and watch for the temptations to which people have succumbed. The terrible covetousness, the liberty without responsibility, the life-styles that flaunt the Sixth Commandment, the blatant voice of the gay world, the promiscuity, the greed, the self-serving—it's all there. It repeats itself in all the media—books, magazines, television shows, radio disc jockeys. Indeed, your adversary the devil walks about as a wolf in sheep's clothing. Your mission is to live in Christ, above these things, beyond these things, without these things. How else can you by your life make a witness to Christ who lives in you? How else can you make a witness with your words?

With the ears of faith listen—you can hear the sound of the wind in the city. Look with the eyes of faith—you can see the tongues of fire above the heads of God's people. Pentecost is not only a feast to celebrate. Pentecost is a daily celebration of the Holy Spirit in the world and in your life. Let your little flame so shine that men may know the Father and the Lord Jesus. Honor the role of martyrs who made the faith possible for you. Pray for the church (which is the people of God), that it may continue its purpose of bringing Christ to the world and peace to the nations and the comfort which is in Christ to every soul.